THE

BABYLON

CONNECTION?

By

Ralph Woodrow

THE BABYLON CONNECTION?

By

Ralph Woodrow

Second printing, January 1999
Third printing, March 2004

International Standard Book Number: 0-916938-17-4.

For a catalog of books and tapes, contact:

RALPH WOODROW
P. O. Box 21,
PALM SPRINGS, CA 92263-0021 USA

Toll free order line: (877) 664-1549
Fax: (760) 323-3982
Email: ralphwoodrow@earthlink.net
Website: www.ralphwoodrow.org

CHAPTERS

INTRODUCTION

In my earlier Christian experience, certain literature fell into my hands which claimed paganism had been mixed into Christianity. While the Roman Catholic Church was usually the target, it seemed other churches had also been contaminated by customs and beliefs for which pagan parallels could be found.

The Two Babylons by Alexander Hislop (1807-1862), with its alarming subtitle, THE PAPAL WORSHIP PROVED TO BE THE WORSHIP OF NIMROD AND HIS WIFE, was *the* textbook on which much of this teaching was based. Over the years, this book has impacted the thinking of many people—ranging all the way from those in radical cults to very dedicated Christians who hunger for a move of God and are concerned about anything that might hinder that flow. Its basic premise is that the pagan religion of ancient Babylon has continued to our day, in disguise, as the Roman Catholic Church and is described in the book of Revelation as "Mystery Babylon the Great"—thus, the idea of *two* Babylons, one ancient, and one modern. Because this book is very detailed, having a multitude of notes and references, I assumed, as did many others, it was factual. We quoted "Hislop" as an authority on paganism, just like "Webster" might be quoted on word definitions.

As a young evangelist I began to share a sermon on the mixture of paganism into Christianity, and eventually wrote a book based on Hislop—*Babylon Mystery Religion*. In time, my book became quite popular, went through many printings, and was translated into Korean, German, Spanish, Portuguese, and several other languages. I came to be regarded by some as an authority on the subject of pagan mixture. Even a noted Roman Catholic writer, Karl Keating, said: "Its best-known proponent is Ralph Woodrow, author of *Babylon Mystery Religion*."[1]

Many preferred my book over *The Two Babylons* because it was easier to read and follow. Sometimes the two books were

1. Keating, *Catholicism and Fundamentalism*, p. 157.

confused with each other, and I even had the experience, on one occasion, of being greeted as "Rev. Hislop"! Letters in a steady flow were received praising my book. Only occasionally would there be a dissenting voice. One who disagreed was Scott Klemm, a high school history teacher in southern California. Being a Christian, and appreciating other things I had written, he began to show me evidence that Hislop was not a reliable historian. As a result, I realized that I needed to go back through Hislop's work, my basic source, and prayerfully check it out!

As I did this, it became clear—Hislop's "history" was often only mythology. Even though myths may sometimes reflect events that actually happened, an arbitrary piecing together of ancient myths can not provide a sound basis for history. Take enough tribes, enough tales, enough time, jump from one time to another, from one country to another, pick and choose similarities—why anything could be "proved"!

The concern about not having anything pagan in our lives can be likened to a ship crossing a vast ocean. This concern has taken us in the right direction, but as we come to a better understanding as to what is actually pagan and what is not, a correction of the course is necessary in our journey. This is not a going back, but a correction of the course as we follow "the shining light, that shines more and more unto the perfect day" (Prov. 4:18).

In the following pages, though we will challenge some of Hislop's claims, this is not intended as an attack against him personally. In addition to being a writer, he served as the pastor of the East Free Church, Arbroath, Scotland. As far as we know, he was a dedicated Christian, a brother in Christ. When we will repeatedly refer to him simply as "Hislop," rather than Rev. Hislop or Mr. Hislop, no lack of respect is intended. Nor is it our goal in writing this book to merely discredit another book. Instead, it is our desire that this effort will help us understand "the way of God more perfectly" (cf. Acts 18:26), find a Biblical balance, and glorify Him who said: "I am the way, the truth, and the life: no man cometh unto the Father, but by me" (John 14:6).

—RALPH WOODROW

Chapter One

BABYLONIAN RELIGION?

Suppose we could go back in time—back to the days of ancient Babylon. What kind of religion would we find being practiced there?

According to Alexander Hislop, we would find people attending mass, partaking of a little round wafer, worshipping a cross, going to confession, being baptized with water for the remission of sins, burning wax candles, and bowing before a divine Mother and Child. We would notice that places of worship featured a tower. Priests, wearing a circular tonsure, dressed in black garments, would give those who died the last rites. With monks and nuns in abundance, the Babylonians would be practicing essentially all the rites that are known today in the Roman Catholic Church!

"Popery boasts of being the 'old religion;' and truly...it is ancient indeed," Hislop says. "It can trace its lineage far beyond the era of Christianity, back over 4000 years, to near the period of the Flood and the building of the Tower of Babel."[1] "The essential character of her system, the grand objects of her worship, her festivals, her doctrine and discipline, her rites and ceremonies, her priesthood and their orders, have *all* been derived from ancient Babylon."[2] If Belshazzar were to come back to life, "and enter St. Peter's at Rome...he would conclude that he had only entered one of his own well-known temples, and that *all things continued as they were at Babylon"!*[3]

According to Hislop, it all started with Nimrod and his wife Semiramis, thus the subtitle of *The Two Babylons*: THE PAPAL WORSHIP PROVED TO BE THE WORSHIP OF NIMROD AND HIS WIFE. But, any information about Nimrod and Semiramis in history books is, at best, sketchy. In the Bible, Nimrod "the mighty hunter," is only

1. Hislop, *The Two Babylons,* p. 287.   2. Ibid., p. 3.   3. Ibid., p. 218.

1

mentioned *four* times[1]—and his wife is *never* mentioned! Nevertheless, Hislop claims to know all kinds of detailed information about Nimrod and his wife.

According to Hislop, "Nimrod," meaning *subduer of the leopard,* was a skilled leopard tamer.[2] He took a trained leopard with him when he went hunting.[3] As a trophy of his skill, he wore a leopard skin, and was called "The spotted one" by people who were "impressed" by his clothing.[4] On his head he wore bull's horns.[5] He gained fame as a mighty hunter by "ridding the world of monsters"[6] and was called the "Emancipator."[7] For entertainment on his various expeditions, "he was always accompanied by troops of women; and by music and song, and games and revelries."[8] "He led mankind to seek their chief good in sensual enjoyment, and showed them how they might enjoy the pleasures of sin, without any fear of the wrath of a holy God."[9]

According to Hislop, Nimrod was also a skilled horse trainer,[10] and came to be regarded as "the god of horse races."[11] Years later, the Centaur, an imaginary creature among the Greeks, half-man and half-horse, was the symbol of Nimrod's horsemanship.[12] Because of his success as a horse breaker and archer, he even came to be represented in the signs of the Zodiac, as Sagittarius the Archer on a horse![13]

According to Hislop, Nimrod was also a military leader.[14] He knew scientific secrets about magic arts and used what we today call explosives or bombs to defeat his enemies.[15] He became known as the war-god of Babylon,[16] and even his grandson, many years later, was chosen by the Greeks as their god of war.[17]

According to Hislop, when the giants rebelled against Heaven, Nimrod was their acknowledged ringleader.[18] His brothers were the famous Cyclops,[19] who were strange looking creatures with one eye, situated in the middle of their foreheads![20]

According to Hislop, all of the Babylonian Mysteries were formed to glorify Nimrod,[21] which included offering human

---

1. Gen. 10:8, 9; 1 Chron. 1:10; Mic. 5:6. 2. Hislop, p. 44. 3. Ibid. 4. Ibid., p. 47.
5. Ibid., p. 65. 6. Ibid., p. 51. 7. Ibid. 8. Ibid., p. 55. 9. Ibid. 10. Ibid., p. 41. 11. Ibid., p. 42. 12. Ibid., p. 41. 13. Ibid., p. 42. 14. Ibid., p. 37. 15. Ibid., p. 230. 16. Ibid., p. 312. 17. Ibid., p. 246. 18. Ibid., p. 55. 19. Ibid., p. 32. 20. Ibid., p. 229. 21. Ibid., p. 296.

sacrifices. His priests "were required to eat of the human sacrifices"[1] and "infants were the most acceptable offerings at his altar,"[2] so that Nimrod became known "as the great child-devourer."[3]

According to Hislop, "Nimrod...introduced the worship of the serpent"[4] and of fire.[5] The "Serpent of Fire" was the grand object of worship,[6] while Nimrod himself came to be regarded as the fire-god of Babylon.[7] He was also the great patron of Masonic art[8] and the one who "established the sciences of magic and astronomy."[9]

According to Hislop, Nimrod had quite a few "firsts" to his credit. He was the—

"first who bred dogs and leopards for hunting."[10]
"first [who] taught the art of horsemanship."[11]
"first who carried on war against his neighbors."[12]
"first that bore the title of a Shepherd-king."[13]
"first that gathered mankind into communities."[14]
"first of mortals that reigned."[15]
"first that offered idolatrous sacrifices."[16]
"first...that bore the title of Moloch."[17]
"first king after the Flood."[18]
"first that gained fame...as [a Free Mason]."[19]
"first of mankind that was deified."[20]

According to Hislop, Nimrod's father Cush (Gen. 10:8), also played a big part in leading people away from God,[21] and was "the first to whom the name Merodach, 'The great Rebel,' must have been given."[22] He was worshipped at Babylon as "the great sooth-sayer."[23] He was "The Numberer," the "Man of the Moon," who "first discovered numbers, and the art of reckoning, geometry, and astronomy, the games of chess and hazard."[24]

According to Hislop, "Nimrod...fell in love with Semiramis when she was another man's wife."[25] She had come from humble beginnings,[26] and had been brought up to believe in God, but was a backslider,[27] given over to a lifestyle of gross immorality.[28] Choosing her for his queen, they become an odd couple: "Semiramis, the

1. Hislop, p. 232   2. Ibid., p. 231.   3. Ibid.   4. Ibid., p. 298.   5. Ibid., p. 226.   6. Ibid.   7. Ibid., p. 230.   8. Ibid., p. 43.   9. Ibid., p. 67.   10. Ibid., p. 45.   11. Ibid. p. 41. 12. Ibid., p. 23.   13. Ibid., p. 217.   14. Ibid., p. 51.   15. Ibid.   16. Ibid.   17. Ibid., p. 315.   18. Ibid., p. 185.   19. Ibid., p. 43.   20. Ibid., p. 231.   21. Ibid., p. 25.   22. Ibid., p. 28.   23. Ibid., p. 34.   24. Ibid., p. 95.   25. Ibid., p. 298.   26. Ibid., p. 58.   27. Ibid., p. 298.   28. Ibid., p. 229.

most beautiful of women,"[1] was white, with golden hair and blue eyes![2] Nimrod, in sharp contrast, was a big, deformed, "most ugly" negro![3]

According to Hislop, Semiramis, "to whom the 'unbloody sacrifice' of the mass was first offered,"[4] invented soprano singing[5] and, like Nimrod, dressed in a unique way, as when "she put on her own head a bull's head, as the ensign of royalty."[6] She was called "the Mermaid" and he was called "the Merman"[7]—"the god of the sea."[8]

According to Hislop, after Nimrod suffered a violent death, his body was cut into fourteen pieces which were sent to as many regions—places where his false doctrine had spread—where they were buried.[9] But, eventually, all of these pieces were recovered —except one: his phallus. It had been devoured by the Lepidotus, the Phagrus, and the Oxyrhynchus, for which reason these fish are held in abhorrence by the Egyptians.[10]

According to Hislop, Nimrod was killed by Shem, Noah's son.[11] His sudden death caused great shock in his kingdom,[12] but priests, seeking to offset this, taught that his death was entirely voluntary, that he had submitted to it for the benefit of the world.[13] Later, when Semiramis gave birth to a son, Tammuz—supposedly Nimrod reincarnated—he "was worshipped as the *son* of his wife."[14] And so, in various countries of the world, when we find a child worshipped in the arms of a goddess-mother, that child is none other than Nimrod![15]

According to Hislop, "Semiramis gained glory from her dead and deified husband" and they were both worshipped as the Mother and Son with an incredible enthusiasm, and their images set up and adored.[16] "Wherever the negro aspect of Nimrod was found an obstacle to his worship, this was very easily obviated" by teaching that he had been reincarnated into a child with "a fair complexion, supernaturally borne by his widowed wife after the father had gone to glory"![17] In time Nimrod was "deposed from his original pre-eminence...on account of his ugliness. Even in Babylon itself, the

1. Hislop, p. 229.   2. Ibid., p. 85.   3. Ibid., p. 229.   4. Ibid., p. 219.   5. Ibid., p. 156.   6. Ibid., p. 264.   7. Ibid.   8. Ibid., p. 41.   9. Ibid., p. 179.   10. Ibid.   11. Ibid., p. 63.   12. Ibid., p. 57.   13. Ibid., p. 62.   14. Ibid., p. 305.   15. Ibid., p. 50.   16. Ibid., p. 69.   17. Ibid.

posthumous child, as identified with his father, and inheriting all his father's glory, yet possessing *more of his mother's complexion* came to be the favorite."[1]

According to Hislop, Semiramis survived her husband forty-two years,[2] finally meeting her fate when one of her sons cut off her head![3] After her death, she was worshipped under the form of a dove or pigeon, having been exalted to divinity.[4] And so, "the first deified woman was no doubt Semiramis, as the first deified man was her husband."[5]

Such is an outline, *according to Hislop,* of the history of Nimrod and his wife. By now the reader may be asking the obvious question: Where does Hislop get all this information? The answer is clear. Based on mere similarities, he merges a variety of mythological stories together so that the hero in each becomes Nimrod:

The Bible says Nimrod was "a mighty one"; in mythology, Hercules was a mighty one or giant—*so Hercules must have been Nimrod!* Nimrod was known as "a mighty hunter"; in mythology, Orion is called the Hunter—*so Orion must have been Nimrod!* The building of the tower of Babel is commonly linked with Nimrod; in mythology, Kronos was the king of the Cyclops who invented tower-building—*so Kronos must have been Nimrod!*

In the accompanying drawing of Bacchus,[6] the wine cup symbolizes his status as god of drunken revelry. But Hislop claims a deeper meaning —that "the name of a cup, in the sacred language, was Khus," or Cush. Figuring the branch is also a symbol, "the two symbols, then, must be read together," he says, and read in this way, they are the equivalent of saying that Bacchus was the "Branch [son] of Cush"![7] Nimrod was the son of Cush (Gen. 10:8)—so, according to Hislop, *Bacchus must have been Nimrod!*

1. Hislop, pp. 69, 70.   2. Ibid., p. 6.   3. Ibid., p. 265.   4. Ibid., p. 78.   5. Ibid., p. 304.
6. Ibid., p. 48.   7. Ibid., pp. 48, 49.

5

Hislop draws attention to "the spots on the robe" of Bacchus[1] and offers the following speculation: "When Nimrod, as 'the Leopard-tamer,' began to be clothed in the leopard-skin, as the trophy of his skill, his spotted dress and appearance must have impressed the imaginations of those who saw him; and he came to be called...'The spotted one'."[2]   And who could this spotted one be but Osiris, as shown in the accompanying drawing? Hislop says "this negro-featured Osiris is clothed from head to foot in a spotted dress, the upper part being a leopard's skin, the under part also being spotted to correspond with it," for which there must be a special meaning.[3] "And what could that meaning be, but just  to identify Osiris with the Babylonian god, who was celebrated as the 'Leopard-tamer'."[4] *So Osiris must have been Nimrod!*

Next Hislop shows the accompanying drawing, "a divinity bearing a spotted fawn," and even though it is a deer and not a leopard, to Hislop the similarity—the spots—make this a symbol of Nimrod also![5] With about as much logic, we might argue that this divinity is wearing a wristwatch on each arm—a real two-timer!

Nimrod gathered people into communities (Gen. 10:10); according to legend, Hislop points out, Phoroneus was the first that gathered mankind into communities[6]—*so Phoroneus must have been Nimrod!*

1. Hislop, p. 49.   2. Ibid., p. 47.   3. Ibid., p. 44.   4. Ibid., p. 46.   5. Ibid. p. 47.
6. Ibid., p. 51

6

Phoroneus was regarded as the inventor of fire, so Nimrod must have been the fire-god! And who could this be but Moloch (Lev. 18:21)? Children were burned in a fire as sacrifices to Moloch (Jer. 7:31), so in the Babylonian mysteries, children were burned in honor of *Nimrod!* Such is the Hislop logic.

On and on it goes, until—according to Hislop—all of the following names or titles refer to Nimrod!

Adonis. "Nimrod...or Adonis of Babylon, was the great war-god" (p. 312).

Aesculapius. "Aesculapius...was evidently just another name for the great Babylonian god [Nimrod]" (p. 236).

Ala-Mahozim. "The name 'Ala-Mahozim'...can be traced home to Nimrod" (p. 296).

Alorus. "Alorus, or the 'god of fire,' that is, Nimrod" (p. 243).

Apollo. "The sun-god Apollo had been known under the name of Lat....the Great Babylonian god [Nimrod]" (p. 270).

Baal. "The priests of Nimrod or Baal..." (p. 232).

Baal-aberin. "Nimrod...was Baal-aberin" (p. 37).

Bacchus. "Nimrod has been proved to be Bacchus" (p. 114).

Bassareus. "Bassareus...was Nimrod, the son of Cush" (p. 50).

Belus. "Belus, that is Nimrod..." (p. 54).

Bol-Kahn. "Nimrod...was Bol-Khan, Priest of Baal" (p. 229).

Centaurus. "Centaurus was the same as...Nimrod" (p. 42).

Chusorus. "The second person of the Phenician trinity was Chusorus...Chus-zoro, The seed of Cush" (p. 50).

Consus. "Consus...patron of horsemanship...the great huntsman of Babel" (p. 41).

Dagon. "Invincible was Nimrod when he reappeared as Dagon, the beast from the sea" (p. 246).

Dayyad. "Dayyad the hunter...evidently Nimrod" (p. 34).

Dionysus. "Dionysus...is, by ancient inquirers, expressly identified with the Egyptian Osiris," or Nimrod (pp. 46, 56).

7

E-anush. "The name E-anush...was applied to the Babylonian Messiah [Nimrod]" (p. 272).

Guebres. "Nimrod...the first of those 'Mighty ones'...under the name of Guebres" (p. 33).

Hephaistos. "Hephaistos...the ringleader in the first rebellion [Nimrod]" (pp. 27, 28).

Hercules. "The Assyrian Hercules...Nimrod the giant" (p. 34).

Janus. "Nimrod...was Saturn"; "Saturn...was identical with Janus" (pp. 269, 271).

Janus Matutinus. "...the same as...Nimrod" (p. 318).

Kentaurus. "The whole history of the primitive Kentaurus entirely agrees with the history of Nimrod" (p. 297).

Khons. "Khons...signifies The Huntsman...Nimrod" (p. 40).

Khuk-hold. "Nimrod, as universal king...Khuk-hold" (p. 229).

Kronos. "Nimrod...Father of the gods, was...Kronos" (p. 231).

Lateinos. "Nimrod was Saturn...Saturn and Lateinos are just synonymous...the same god" (pp. 269, 270).

Latus. "Latus...another name for the fish-god Dagon"; "Nimrod...reappeared as Dagon" (pp. 270, 246).

Linus. "Linus was the same god as...Osiris of Egypt"; "the Egyptian Osiris...was Nimrod" (pp. 22, 56).

Lucifer. "Lucifer, who was cast down...is the same as...Nimrod" (p. 318).

Mamers. "Nimrod was...Mamers" (p. 44).

Mars. "The original of Mars was Nimrod" (p. 297).

Mavors. "[Mavors] the Roman god of war is just the name of Nimrod..." (p. 246).

Melikerta. "Melikerta...is the same as...Nimrod" (p. 318).

Memmon. "Memmon and Osiris were only different names of the same divinity"; "Osiris was Nimrod" (pp. 22, 56).

Merodach. "Nimrod was a rebel...Merodach" (p. 44).

Mithra. "Nimrod...the Sun-god...Mithra" (p. 194).

8

Moloch. "Nimrod, the god of fire...Moloch" (p. 229).

Mulciber. "Mulciber...or Nimrod" (p. 296).

Nar-kissos. "Nar-kissos is 'The child of Cush'...." (p. 156).

Nebrod. "The name of Nimrod, as known to the Greeks, was Nebrod" (p. 47).

Ninus. "Ninus, Nimrod, and Zoroaster were one" (p. 314).

Oannes. "Nimrod was called, when he reappeared in the Mysteries...Oannes" (p. 114).

Orion. "Orion...that 'mighty hunter'...was Nimrod" (p. 305).

Orpheus. "Orpheus is just a synonym for...the great Babylonian god [Nimrod]" (p. 124).

Osiris. "The identity of Nimrod...and the Egyptian Osiris, having been established..." (p. 56).

Phaëthon. "Nimrod...was represented under the well-known name of Phaëthon" (p. 230).

Phoroneus. "Phoroneus, whom we have identified with Nimrod..." (p. 227).

Pluto. "The name Pluto is only a synonym for Saturn" or Nimrod (pp. 153, 31).

Saturn. "Nimrod...as the god of the Chaldean Mysteries...was Saturn" (p. 269).

Tahmurs. "Tahmurs, who built Babylon...could be none other than Nimrod" (p. 45).

Tammuz. "Tammuz...in other words Nimrod" (p. 228).

Tithonus. "Tithonus...the same as 'the mighty hunter' of Scripture" (p. 317).

Vulcan. "Vulcan, whose identity with Nimrod is shown..." (p. 70).

Wodan. "Wodan...can be proved to be the Adon of Babylon" who was the same as Nimrod (pp. 134, 312).

Zer-Nebo-Gus. "Zer-Nebo-Gus, the great 'seed of the prophet Cush,' was, of course, Nimrod" (p. 34).

Zoroaster. "Zoroaster was...the founder of the idolatrous system of Babylon, and therefore Nimrod" (p. 59).

9

But Hislop's method of mixing myths together, so that Nimrod "occupies so large a place,"[1] cannot be a sound basis on which to build history. It builds on a few similarities, while ignoring vast differences!

By this method, one could argue that Peter and Paul were the same person! Each was an Israelite. Each lived at the same time. Each had a Jewish background. Each was a convert to Christ. Each was an apostle. Each was a Biblical writer. Each suffered martyrdom. And each name begins with the letter "P." But they were two different people!

By this method, one could link the 12 sons of Jacob with the 12 signs of the Zodiac! Comparing the prophetic utterances Jacob gave over his sons (Genesis 49), it could be said that:

Reuben, "unstable as *water*" (verse 4)—was Aquarius, represented as a man pouring out *water*; Judah, a *"lion"* (verse 9)—was Leo the *lion;* Dan, "that *bites* the horse heels" (verse 17)—was the Scorpion, represented as *biting* the heel of the Archer's horse; Gad (verse 19), spelled backward, *dag,* the Hebrew word for fish—was Pisces the Fish; Asher, "his *bread* shall be fat" (verse 20)—corresponded with Virgo, represented as holding a full ear of grain from which *bread* is made; Naphtali, by a play on his name, *taleh,* the *ram* (verse 21)—was Aries the *Ram;* Joseph, "his *bow* remains in strength" (verse 24)—was Sagittarius, the *Archer;* Benjamin, "a ravening *wolf*" (verse 27)—was Capricorn the Goat, sometimes shown with the head of a *wolf,* etc.

These few similarities, however, hardly make the case! If one takes a closer look, there are many differences. We don't believe Jacob was practicing some form of occult astrology!

Years from now, Roy Rogers will be remembered for his western movies as King of the Cowboys, Will Rogers as a cowboy philosopher, and Jimmy Rogers as the Father of Country Music. Basing ideas on a few similarities, someone could write a book claiming these three men were one and the same. Each was an American. Each lived in the twentieth century. Each had the name Rogers. But *differences* would make it clear they were three different individuals!

1. Hislop, p. 295.

10

Take enough stories, enough names, enough centuries, translate from one language to another, and a careless writer of the future might pass on all kinds of misinformation. Gerald Ford, the American President, might be confused with Henry Ford, the car manufacturer. Abraham Lincoln might end up as the inventor of the automobile, the proof being that many cars had the name "Lincoln." Ralph Woodrow the preacher, if remembered at all, might be confused with Woodrow Wilson the president. I have received letters addressed to the "Woodrow Wilson Evangelistic Association"!

Billy Graham has received mail addressed to Billy Sunday. Because his wife's maiden name is Bell, she has sometimes been called Ruth Bell Graham. The inventor of the telephone was Alexander Graham Bell. By mixing up names, someone might end up saying Billy Graham was the inventor of the telephone! Or that he invented Graham Crackers! But in fact, the inventor of Graham Crackers was Sylvester Graham. Again, similarities could be pointed out. Each man was named Graham. Each man was a minister. But the differences make a difference: Sylvester was a Presbyterian and Billy a Baptist!

As was the case with Nimrod, so Hislop finds similarities between various goddesses, and on this basis, supposes all of them were but different names for Semiramis:

Alma Mater. "Semiramis...was called Alma Mater" (p. 76).

Amarusia. "In Athens she was called Amarusia" (p. 158).

Aphrodité. "Aphrodité...identical with...Semiramis" (p. 75).

Artemis. "Semiramis the same as the goddess Artemis" (p. 30).

Asht-trt. "The woman that made towers [Semiramis]" (p. 75).

Astarte. "Astarte is identified with Semiramis" (p. 307).

Atergatis. "Atergatis, the fish goddess...was sometimes identified with Semiramis" (p. 86).

Athor. "Semiramis...was styled Athor" (p. 77).

Aurora. "The name Aurora, given to the wife of...that 'mighty hunter'...Nimrod" (p. 305).

11

Bellona. "The name given to the goddess...[Nimrod's] wife—i.e. Bellona" (p. 44).

Beltis. "She [was called] Beltis, My lady" (p. 264).

Bona Dea. "In Rome she was called Bona Dea" (p. 158).

Ceres. "Ceres...the same as the great goddess of Babylon" (p. 76).

Cybele. "In Asia [the Mother-goddess was known] as Cybele" (p. 20).

Derketo. "[The Mother-goddess was called] Derketo, the Mermaid" (p. 264).

Diana. "Diana...was identified with Semiramis" (p. 30).

Dione. "Dione, as meaning Venus, is clearly applied...to the Babylonian goddess" (p. 78).

Easter. "Easter, the goddess queen of Babylon..." (p. 110).

Irene. "Irene, the goddess of Peace...the original of that mother...was Semiramis" (pp. 20, 21).

Isis. The "Goddess Mother...in Egypt [was worshipped as] Isis" (p. 20).

Juno. "Semiramis...worshipped as Juno, the Dove" (p. 141).

Melkat-ashemin. "As the Moon-goddess [she was called] Melkat-ashemin, Queen of heaven" (p. 264).

Melissa. "A title of Semiramis...Melissa" (p. 310).

Mylitta. "In Babylon she bore the name of Mylitta—that is, The Mediatrix" (p. 157).

Myrionymus. "Nimrod...his wife...Myrionymus" (p. 269).

Pambasileia. "[The Mother-goddess] Pambasileia, Queen of the universe" (p. 265).

Pessinuntica. "Pessinuntica [was the same as] Venus" or Semiramis (pp. 302, 75).

Proserpine. "Proserpine with whom...the Babylonian goddess ...was identified" (p. 126).

Rhea. "Semiramis...was worshipped...under the name of Rhea" (p. 21).

Sacca. "The title of the goddess-mother...was Sacca" (p. 78).

Semelé. "The name by which she was now known was Semelé" (p. 265).

Shing Moo. "Shing Moo is just a synonym for one of the well-known names of the goddess-mother of Babylon" (p. 294).

Venus. "Venus...is none other than...Semiramis" (p. 75).

Vesta. "Semiramis...the Babylonian queen...had the name of...Vesta" (p. 77).

And so, by citing similarities, and ignoring differences, Hislop supposes that all kinds of goddesses were but variations of one goddess—a deified Semiramis of Babylon! But by this method, one could conclude that Mary Baker Eddy, Ellen G. White, and Aimee Semple McPherson were the same woman!

All three were instrumental in establishing a religious denomination. But there are distinct differences between The Church of Christ, Scientist; the Seventh-Day Adventist Church; and the International Church of the Foursquare Gospel! All taught healing, but with different methods: Mary Baker Eddy emphasized the mind, Ellen G. White diet, and Aimee Semple McPherson faith.

All three wrote books. But there are distinct differences between *Science and Health, The Great Controversy,* and *This is That.* All three lived in America, but at different places: Boston, Battle Creek, and Los Angeles. All three lived close enough in time that their lives overlapped, yet there were differences: Mary Baker Eddy (1821-1910), Ellen G. White (1826-1915), and Aimee Semple McPherson (1890-1944).

When Mrs. Eddy died, final burial in the Mount Auburn Cemetery was delayed while a suitable tomb was constructed. During this time, the coffin was placed in a nearby building and guarded day and night. Because a telephone was installed for the convenience of the guards, a rumor circulated that Mrs. Eddy was buried with a telephone, should she awaken and need it![1]

---

1. Silberger, *Mary Baker Eddy—An Interpretive Biography of the Founder of Christian Science,* p. 240.

13

Later the story transferred to Aimee McPherson—that *she* had been buried with a live telephone! This was once a question on the "Hollywood Squares" television program. Of course it is not true. I have a personal letter from Rolf K. McPherson showing how unfounded the rumor about his mother is. Forest Lawn cemetery has issued a letter pointing out there are no phone lines in that part of the cemetery and never have been. I am familiar with Forest Lawn in that my wife's grandmother, a dedicated Christian lady, is also buried there. The whole telephone rumor is ridiculous, but it illustrates how similarities can lead to confusion!

SEMIRAMIS AND VENUS

An example of such confusion may be seen in Hislop's claim that Semiramis was the same as Venus—who was hatched from an egg! According to a fable, this egg of wondrous size fell from heaven into the river Euphrates, fish rolled it to the bank, doves settled on it, hatched it, and out came the goddess Venus![1] When

condemning Easter eggs, Hislop uses this egg as an *evil* symbol, but here he gives it a *good* meaning: that this wondrous egg, from which Venus or Semiramis came, was *Noah's ark!*

By jumping from one culture to another, from one time to another, and from one language to another, Hislop tries to explain. He says the "Hindoos" spoke of a *mundane* egg; "mundane" means *world,* so this must refer to Noah's family within the ark (egg) by whom the world would again be populated. The Hebrew

1. Hislop, p. 109.

14

word for "egg" is *baitz,* which in its feminine form is *baitza,* which "in Chaldee" becomes *baitha,* which is the way *house* was pronounced. And so, he says: "The egg floating on the waters that contained the world, was the *house* floating on the waters of the deluge....The coming of the egg from heaven evidently refers to the preparation of the ark by express appointment of God....The doves resting on the egg need no explanation."[1]

Hislop feels "no explanation" is needed about the doves—we all know, of course, that Noah sent forth a dove from the ark—but where is the connection? In the fable, the egg fell into the Euphrates *river,* whereas the surface on which the ark floated was a vast *flood.*

But having set forth the teaching that the wondrous egg represents Noah's ark, Hislop faces the dilemma of Venus or Semiramis coming out of the egg (ark). Was Semiramis in the ark? To explain this, he speculates even more:

Though the deified queen [Semiramis]...had no actual existence till some centuries after the flood, yet through the doctrine of *metempsychosis* [reincarnation]...it was easy for her worshippers to be made to believe that, in a previous incarnation, she had lived in the Antediluvian world, and passed in safety through the waters of the flood.[2]

To us, this seems like needless labor to make a point that proves nothing. While on one hand Hislop speaks against the mixtures that have gone on in Roman Catholicism, yet he has specialized in his own brand of mixture: the mixing of myths.

BAPTISMAL REGENERATION?

Typical of this myth mixing is the way Hislop seeks to show that the Babylonians practiced "baptismal regeneration." Because rites involving water for ritual cleansing or regeneration were practiced in various countries, he assumes this was also the practice in Babylon. But what would be the *basis* for the Babylonians practicing baptismal regeneration? As he pondered this question, he came up with the theory that it tied in with Noah's flood! Admittedly, this would have some similarity: baptism involves water; the flood involved water! But where is the connection?

1. Hislop, p. 110.   2. Ibid.

15

Hislop labors long here with bits and pieces of mythology, leading us through a maze of speculation. He gives the accompanying illustration of "Diphues" (meaning "twice-born"), a god with two heads. This, he says, must have been Noah who—because of the flood —lived in two worlds, and so looked backward and forward.[1] He points out that the god Janus is also pictured with two heads, and in one of the "mixed up" legends, was "the inventor of ships."[2] So, he reasons, Noah, Diphues, and Janus must have been one and the same!

Next, Hislop takes us to India, where a legend regarding the god Vishnu (who slept four months every year) speaks of one righteous family being miraculously preserved when the world was drowned. The name Vishnu, he says, is "the Sanskrit form of the Chaldee Ish-nuh," *Ish* meaning man and *nuh* meaning Noah![3] A similar name in mythology, Ishnu, was the god of *rain*.[4] I suppose the intended connection is *rain*—it rained at the time of Noah!

Hislop tells us that the name Saturn means "the hidden one," and since Noah was *hidden* in the ark, Saturn must be another name for Noah![5] Amassing even more "proof," he cites the myth of the Egyptian Osiris who was "shut up in his coffin" and set afloat on the Nile on "the 17th day of the month Athyr."[6] Because it was also the 17th day of the month when Noah entered the ark (Gen. 7:11), further linkage is claimed: the "coffin" of Osiris becomes the ark, and Osiris Noah. Ultimately, when Noah (Osiris) came forth from the ark (coffin), where he had been hidden for a year on the waters, it was a sign of new life or regeneration. And so, Hislop speculates:

> The Chaldean priests...led their votaries to believe that, if they only passed through the baptismal waters, and the penances therewith connected, that of itself would make them like the second father of mankind, 'Diphues,' 'twice-born,' or 'regenerated,' would entitle them to all the privileges of 'righteous' Noah, and give them that 'new birth.'[7]

1. Hislop, p. 134.   2. Ibid., p. 135, quoting from Bryant's *Mythology,* Vol. iii, p. 78.
3. Ibid., p.135.   4. Ibid.   5. Ibid., p. 136.   6. Ibid.   7. Ibid., p. 137.

16

To us, this is a very strained attempt to show that baptismal regeneration was practiced in Babylon! But Hislop not only makes this claim, he even insists this is the source from which the Roman Catholic Church obtained its doctrine:

> From this very source has its doctrine of baptismal regeneration been derived...this, *and this only,* will be found to be the real origin of the anti-Scriptural dogma....Papal baptism is just a reproduction of the Chaldean.[1]

Yet with all of this, he has never once shown that baptismal regeneration was actually practiced in Babylon! If Roman Catholic leaders got the idea from Babylon, one wonders what book they read that gave them this idea.

If a pagan book had said, "Arise, and be baptized, and wash away thy sins," Hislop would have jumped on this as being from Babylon! Yet these words are not from some Babylonian book, but from the Bible itself! (Acts 22:16). For those of us, as believers in Jesus Christ, who believe in Christian baptism, it should be obvious there is an inherent weakness in Hislop's whole argument against baptismal *regeneration:* the same basic arguments could be used against water baptism in general.

Hislop's claims get even wilder when he says the Babylonians believed they could be regenerated by baptism because *Nimrod and Semiramis had suffered for them!*

To arrive at this conclusion, Hislop starts by telling about a Mr. Hogan of Philadelphia who published an account of why he left the Roman Catholic Church, and who consequently had the following curse pronounced on him: "May the Father, who creates man, curse him! May the Son, who suffered for us, curse him! May the *Holy Ghost who suffered for us in baptism,* curse him!"[2]

Hislop supposes these words about the Holy Ghost suffering in baptism refer to Nimrod's wife, Semiramis! Turning again to mythology, he says that after Semiramis was exalted to divinity, she came to be worshipped as Juno, the "Dove."[3] Because the dove is linked with the Holy Ghost (Lk. 3:22), he reasons that Semiramis became a counterfeit of the Holy Ghost!

1. Hislop, pp. 137.   2. Ibid., p. 141.   3. Ibid., p.141.

Next, claiming that Semiramis was the same as Venus, Hislop cites the words of Manilius—that "Venus plunged into the Babylonian waters to shun the fury of the snake-footed Typhon."[1] And so, he reasons, this "was neither more nor less than saying that the Holy Ghost incarnate in deep tribulation entered these waters, and...by the Spirit's efficacy thus imparted to them, for giving new life and regeneration, by baptism, to the worshippers of the Chaldean Madonna....When, therefore, we read...that 'the Holy Ghost suffered for us in baptism,' surely it must now be manifest who is that Holy Ghost that is really intended. *It is no other than Semiramis*."[2] Hislop really loses us on this one.

But not only did Semiramis suffer in the waters, according to Hislop, *Nimrod* did also. He cites lines from Homer regarding Bacchus: "In a mad mood, while Bacchus blindly raged...in fearful dissipation...lost in wild dismay...plunged in the deep."[3] By making Nimrod and Bacchus one and the same, *Nimrod plunged in the deep!* And so, on evidence no stronger than this, he concludes: "The worshippers of Nimrod and his queen were looked upon as regenerated and purged from sin by baptism, which baptism received its virtue *from the sufferings of these two great Babylonian divinities*."[4] What? Babylonians believed Nimrod and his queen suffered for them so they could be purged from sin by being baptized? This is wild speculation!

Bearing in mind that Hislop's subtitle is: THE PAPAL WORSHIP PROVED TO BE THE WORSHIP OF NIMROD AND HIS WIFE, I have carefully checked the articles on "Nimrod" and "Semiramis" in many recognized reference works, including the following:

The Encyclopedia Americana
The Encyclopedia Britannica
The Encyclopedia Judaica
The Encyclopedia of Religion
The New Catholic Encyclopedia
The World Book Encyclopedia

NOT ONE SAYS ANYTHING ABOUT NIMROD AND SEMIRAMIS BEING HUSBAND AND WIFE!

---

1. Hislop, p. 143.   2. Ibid., pp. 141-144.   3. Ibid., p. 142.   4. Ibid., p. 144.

Not only is there no mention of Nimrod being married to Semiramis, the information given tends to rule this out entirely. *The Encyclopedia Britannica* and *The Encyclopedia Americana* say Semiramis or Sammu-ramat, as she was called by the Assyrians, was the wife of Shamshi-Adad V who reigned 823-811 B.C. Nimrod, by all accounts, would have lived much earlier than this!

Some scholars have identified Nimrod with Sargon the Great, who lived about 2600 B.C.; others with Gilgamesh the heroic figure of about 2200 B.C.; others with the Egyptian monarch Amenophis III of about 1411; and still others with king Tukulti-Ninurta I about 1246 B.C.[1] If this information is correct, instead of Nimrod and Semiramis being husband and wife, *they did not even live in the same century!*

History about Semiramis is so confused, some have supposed there were two women by this name, and that one may have lived earlier. That there is uncertainty about the dating, Hislop admits.[2] He says she was married to Ninus, whom he supposes was Nimrod. But as Layard (often quoted by Hislop) says:

> With regard to the historical Semiramis, the *confusion* as to the time of her existence, her deeds, and her connection with Ninus, is equally *inexplicable*. She is declared to be the wife, daughter, and even the mother, or step-mother, of that monarch.[3]

There is no need to even try to unravel any of this, for information this confused and inexplicable cannot provide any sound basis for arguments about Roman Catholicism!

If we sought to base an argument on George Washington and his wife, we could at least start out with facts. We could show who George Washington was, that he had a wife named Martha, when they lived—and continue from there. *But,* if no historian was certain who George Washington was, or if he even had a wife, or when they lived, this would not be a sound basis on which to prove anything! Such is the inherent weakness of Hislop's thesis that papal worship is the worship of Nimrod and his wife.

1. *New Illustrated Bible Dictionary*, article: "Nimrod"; *The Encyclopedia Americana,* article: "Nimrod." 2. Hislop, p. 6. 3. Layard, *Nineveh and its Remains,* p. 480.

An article in "The Saturday Review," dated September 17, 1859, written just after the second edition of Hislop's book was published, said this:

> In the first place, his whole superstructure is raised upon nothing. Our earliest authority for the history of Semiramis wrote about the commencement of the Christian era, and the historian from whom he drew his information lived from fifteen hundred to two thousand years after the date which Mr. Hislop assigns to the great Assyrian Queen. The most lying legend which the Vatican has ever endorsed stands on better authority than the history which is now made the ground of a charge against it.
>
> Secondly, the whole argument proceeds upon the assumption that all heathenism has a common origin. Accidental resemblances in mythological details are taken as evidence of this, and nothing is allowed for the natural working of the human mind.
>
> Thirdly, Mr. Hislop's method of reasoning would make anything of anything. By the aid of obscure passages in third-rate historians, groundless assumptions of identity, and etymological torturing of roots, all that we know, and all that we believe, may be converted...into something totally different.
>
> Fourthly, Mr. Hislop's argument proves too much. He finds not only the corruptions of Popery, but the fundamental articles of the Christian Faith, in his hypothetical Babylonian system...
>
> We take leave of Mr. Hislop and his work with the remark that we never before quite knew the folly of which ignorant or half-learned bigotry is capable.[1]

Hislop's method of trying to produce a "history" based on mythology is often contradictory. On page 78 of *The Two Babylons,* Nimrod's wife was his *daughter!* On page 44 she was his *sister!* On page 317 she was his *mother!* On page 307, Bacchus (supposedly the same as Nimrod) is called "Bimater"—a man with *two* mothers! On page 76, an unrelated myth from Scandinavia is introduced, about Heimdal, "the son of nine virgins"! How much more mixed-up can it get? This is not deep truth; this is nonsense!

---

1. "The Saturday Review," Sept. 17, 1859, p. 340.

Hislop says Nimrod was the "Father of the gods"; Cush, Nimrod's father, was the "Father of the gods"; Kronos was the "Father of the gods"—all of these statements being found on page 32! On page 277 he says Pluto, the god of Hell, was the "Father of the gods." On page 164 he says Seb was the "Father of the gods." On page 27 he says Vulcan was the "Father of the gods." On page 299 he says Saturn was the "Father of gods," who "was in one aspect just *our first parent Adam"!* Does any of this make sense?

Hislop calls Nimrod's wife the "Mother of the gods"; Rhea is called the "Mother of the gods;" and *Eve* is called the "Mother of the gods"—all on page 304. On page 20, Beltis is called the "Mother of the gods." On page 21 Minerva is called the "Mother of the gods." On page 303, Cybele is called the "Mother of the gods." How could all of these, including *Eve,* be the "Mother of the gods"?

Hislop, claiming that the name Saturn means "The hidden one," concludes that the Devil, Adam, Noah, Nimrod, and Saturn were all one and the same—because each one *hid* in some way: "The different myths about Saturn, when carefully examined, show that he was at once the Devil...who *hid* himself under the disguise of the serpent,—and Adam, who *hid* himself among the trees of the garden,—and Noah, who lay *hid* for a whole year in the ark,—and Nimrod, who was *hid* in the secrecy of the Babylonian Mysteries."[1]

Hislop also says that "Saturn, the hidden god...was identical to Janus."[2] In another place, he says that Janus was Nimrod; Janus was Nimrod's father Cush; and Janus was Nimrod's great grandfather Noah—all on page 135. This reminds me of a humorous song from years past: "I'm My Own Grandpa!"

It is not unusual for Hislop to find similarities between two different *gods* and argue they were one and the same. It is not unusual for him to find similarities between two different *goddesses* and argue they were one and the same. He might argue that the god Janus was the same as Saturn,[3] or that the goddess Cybele was the same as Rhea.[4] But he loses all credibility when he says that Androgyne was *"both Janus and Cybele at the same time,"* having "both sexes"![5]

1. Hislop, p. 296.   2. Ibid., p. 271.   3. Ibid.   4. Ibid., p. 302.   5. Ibid., p. 242.

Surely all of this cries out in a clear voice that a mixture of myths is no basis on which to prove or disprove doctrinal viewpoints! Even Biblical information, if mixed, cannot provide a clear picture of truth. The story is told of a zealous, though uneducated, preacher who covered a lot of ground in his preaching, but he mixed things up:

Once upon a time a man come down from Jerusalem to Jericho an' fell among thieves, an' the thorns growed up an' choked that man. An' he didn't have no money, but he met the Queen of Sheba, an' she gave him a thousand talents of gold, an' a hundred changes of raiment.

An' he went on in a chariot and druv furiously. An' when he was drivin' under a big tree his hair got caught in a limb, an' left him hangin' there. Yes sir, an' the ravens brung him food to eat. One night while he was hangin' there, his wife Delilah come an' cut off his hair, an' he fell on stony ground. It began to rain an' it rained forty days an' forty nights. He would have drowned, but the Lord prepared a great fish to swallow him.

An' he went on and met a man who said, 'Come and take supper with me.' An' he said, 'I cain't, I married a wife.' An' that man went into the highway and the byway an' compelled him to come.

An' he went on and come to Jerusalem, an' he saw Queen Jezebel sittin' high in the window. An' she laughed at him. Amen! He said, 'Throw her down.' And they throwed her down, an' he said, 'Throw her down some more.' An' they throwed her down seventy times seven, and the dogs ate her flesh. Now whose wife will she be in the resurrection?

The point we would make is simply this: mixing Biblical stories cannot provide a valid basis for doctrine—and mixing bits and pieces of mythology cannot provide a valid basis for history.

Chapter Two

BABYLONIAN BEGINNINGS?

"The confessional was borrowed from *Babylon*," Hislop says. "In that system, secret confession to the priest, according to a prescribed form, was required of all who were admitted to the 'Mysteries'."[1] Yet he shows no evidence of any confessional in Babylon, but cites a form of confession—an initiation rite required at the temple of Delphi—in *Greece!*[2]

Over and over Hislop claims that all kinds of things started "in Babylon," yet when it comes right down to it, the examples he gives are usually from some *other country*. He reasons that if a tribe in Africa worshipped a cross, *the cross must have been an object of worship in Babylon!* If the egg was regarded as sacred in China, *the egg was a sacred object in Babylon!* If round cakes were a part of Egyptian rituals, *round cakes were used in Babylon!* If a group practiced baptismal regeneration in Mexico, *baptismal regeneration was practiced in Babylon!* If a mother with child in her arms was worshipped in India, *a mother with child was worshipped in Babylon!*

In other words, we know what the Babylonian religion was, because we find it *somewhere else* in the world. Because we find it somewhere else in the world, we know it came *from Babylon!* This is circular reasoning.

The basic argument is that following the disruption of language at the tower of Babel, people were scattered "upon the face of *all the earth*" (Gen. 11:9), presumably taking their religion with them, where it developed in various forms and names. It is easy to suppose that—"upon the face of all the earth"—means the entire planet. But the word that is here translated "earth," *erets*, is

1. Hislop, p. 9. 2. Ibid.

23

commonly used in a much more limited sense. The following quotation from Genesis 10 and 11 shows how *erets* has sometimes been translated "earth" and other times "land":

> Nimrod...began to be a mighty one in the **earth** [*erets*]....And the beginning of his kingdom was Babel...in the **land** [*erets*] of Shinar....out of that **land** [*erets*] went forth Asshur....And the whole **earth** [*erets*] was of one language....As they journeyed from the east, they found a plain in the **land** [*erets*] of Shinar; and they dwelt there. And they said...let us build us a city and a tower....the Lord did there confound the language of all the **earth** [*erets*]: and from thence did the Lord scatter them abroad upon the face of all the **earth** [*erets*]....And Haran died before his father Terah in the **land** [*erets*] of his nativity, in Ur....And they went forth...into the **land** [*erets*] of Canaan.

There is every reason to believe *erets* should be *uniformly* translated throughout the passage. "Earth," in the sense of the planet, cannot provide a uniform translation, for then we would have absurdity: "the earth of Canaan," "the earth of Shinar," "out of that earth went forth Asshur," etc. The word "land," however, can be used throughout, providing a good sense.

Nimrod, becoming known as "a mighty one in the *earth,*" cannot mean he was famous in places like China, Russia, Mexico, and Australia! His fame was in the *"land* of Shinar," later known as Assyria, "the land [*erets*] of Nimrod" (Mic. 5:6). The Babel builders being scattered abroad upon *all* the face of the *erets,* cannot mean *all* the face of the *planet,* for in vast areas of the planet, at the poles, they would have frozen to death! Everything considered, it is far more likely that the dispersion at Babel involved that part of the world—that *land*—not the entire planet.

Now it is true, of course, that one civilization influences another, but there is no reason to assume that *all* pagan worship is simply a development of ideas that spread from Babylon. Are we to assume that Nimrod and Semiramis invented religious rites, but no one else had any original ideas later on? This is not realistic, for it does not allow room for human ingenuity. There are always some who will rebel against the status quo—whatever it is—and come up with something different.

24

The Bible even mentions that new gods—and consequently new religious ideas—were invented after this time: "...gods whom they knew not...new gods that came newly up, whom your fathers feared not" (Deut. 32:17).

In over 200 verses the Bible mentions pagan "gods," pointing out there are "many" that are called gods (1 Cor. 8:5), and in nearly 300 verses, "Babylon" is mentioned. If all the pagan worship of the "gods" started in "Babylon," as Hislop says, it is strange that in all these verses the Bible never mentions this.

Primitive people who had no contact with each other—or with ancient Babylon—might develop similar practices and beliefs. Because life depends on it, the sun could easily become an object of worship, and for which images could be made. Phases of the moon, as well as seasons, could be used to mark times for festivals. Some rites would develop around sexual acts, cycles, birth, puberty, and death.

The awe that the birth of a baby would inspire, could result in images of a mother with a child in her arms as objects of worship. Ritualistic uses of water and fire might easily find a place. The fact is, many things have been a natural development of religion—totally separate from any supposed Babylonian origin.

Hislop tells of "the Red Indians of America" who in ritual dances wore on their heads buffalo horns,[1] of an obscure divinity in Japan that was pictured with bull's horns and called "The ox-headed Prince of Heaven,"[2] of the mythological god Kronos whose name means "The Horned One,"[3] and of others who wore horns in various ways.[4] Then, typically, he reasons: "We may be sure that such a custom...indicates the wide-spread diffusion of an influence that went forth in all directions *from Babylon*, from the time that Nimrod first 'began to be mighty on the earth'."[5] He assumes, therefore, that *Nimrod wore horns!*[6] The possibility that primitive people might have watched animals fight, with horns clashing, and for this simple reason came to regard horns as a symbol of power, does not seem to cross his mind.

---

1. Hislop, p. 37.   2. Ibid., p. 216.   3. Ibid., p. 33.   4. Ibid.   5. Ibid., p. 37.   6. Ibid., p. 33.

The accompanying drawing of Hercules, from Layard, is described by Hislop—who takes Hercules to mean Nimrod—in the following manner: the figure on the left is Nimrod without weapons

of any kind attacking a bull; having overcome the bull, he sets the bull's horns on his head as a symbol of power. In the second figure he has acquired the legs and feet of the bull and turns to encounter a lion.[1] But when we turn to Hislop's source, Layard says absolutely nothing about Nimrod, but describes this green jasper engraving as representing "the Assyrian Hercules contending with a buffalo, *and* a horned human figure, with the extremities of a bull, fighting with a lion. Between the two groups is an antelope with long spiral horns."[2] Hislop's explanation, then, at best, could only be speculation.

"BEFORE THE LORD"

The Bible says Nimrod was a mighty hunter *"before* the Lord" (Gen. 10:9). There was a time when I took this to mean he put himself *before* the Lord—that he was rebellious *against* the Lord. Augustine apparently took it this way.[3] But "before the Lord" is a *very common* Biblical expression that is repeatedly used of *righteous* people, including Abraham, Isaac, Jacob, Moses, Aaron, Joshua, Samuel, David, Solomon, Hezekiah, and many more.[4] We are not suggesting that Nimrod was a righteous person—though some have considered this possibility[5]—but the major negatives about him have come, not from the Bible, but from Jewish legends.

1. Hislop, p. 34. 2. Layard, *Nineveh and Babylon,* p. 605. 3. Augustine, *The City of God,* 16:4. 4. Gen. 19:27; 27:7; Exod. 16:33; Josh. 18:10; 1 Sam. 2:18; 2 Sam. 5:3; 1 Kings 8:65; 2 Kings 19:14, etc. 5. Kitto, *A Cyclopedia of Biblical Literature,* article: "Nimrod."

According to such legends, Nimrod excited men in contempt of God and gradually turned the government into tyranny, boasting he would build a tower so high it would provide safety if God sent another flood.[1] Nimrod, it is said, had in his possession the original coats of skins that God made for Adam and Eve. These had been passed down to Noah, who took them into the ark, but Ham stole them. Later he passed them on to his son Cush, who in turn passed them on to Nimrod, who wore them when he went hunting. As a result, animals crouched before him, and he caught them without difficulty.[2] According to legend, Nimrod took an army to fight against Abraham, but they were driven away by a swarm of gnats. In one encounter, a gnat flew up Nimrod's nose and gnawed away at his brain![3] These must be the type of stories that Paul referred to as "Jewish fables" (Titus 1:14).

But Hislop carries the Nimrod theme far beyond the Jewish fables, even supposedly finding information about Nimrod in India. According to a legend there, the fifth head of Brahma was cut off. Figuring these heads as a succession, Hislop says that Noah, having lived in two worlds, counts as two heads. His son "Ham is the third, Cush the fourth, and Nimrod is, of course, the fifth" who had his head cut off.[4]

Even in Tahiti, Hislop supposes there is information about Nimrod! A fable is told there about a time when the heavens were so close to earth that men had to crawl. Then someone was able to raise them to the top of the *teve* plant—about four feet high. In another attempt, he lifted them to the height of the *Kauariki* tree. Later he carried them to the summits of the mountains. Finally, after a long interval, he elevated them to their present height. For these accomplishments, he was deified.

Hislop says that Nimrod moved "heaven"—that is, God— away from the people by his false teachings. He then asks: "Now, what could more graphically describe the position of mankind soon after the flood, and the proceedings of Nimrod as Phoroneus, 'The Emancipator,' than this Polynesian fable?"[5] We fail to see any valid connection or point.

1. Josephus, *Antiquities of the Jews*, Book 1, 4:2.   2. *The Jewish Encyclopedia*, article: "Nimrod."   3. Ibid.   4. Hislop, pp. 315, 316.   5. Ibid., p. 53.

If we were to apply this fable to the time of Nimrod, the tower of Babel, in order to "reach unto heaven," would have only needed to be a few feet tall!

TOWER OF BABEL

Once it is assumed that so many things "started in Babylon," it is only another step to speculate that the "tower of Babel" (Gen. 11:4) may have influenced the building of church towers. But from all indications, the tower of Babel was in the form of a *ziggurat,* described by Herodotus (c. 484-c. 425 B.C.) in these words:

> There was a tower of solid masonry...upon which was raised a second tower, and on that a third, and so on up to eight. The ascent to the top is on the outside, by a path which winds round all the towers. When one is about half-way up, one finds a resting-place and seats, where persons are wont to sit some time on their way to the summit. On the topmost tower there is a spacious temple.[1]

This is *not* the design of church towers!

If building a tower is wrong—because of the tower of Babel—building a *city* would also be wrong, for their plan was to build "a *city* and a tower." But even God is called the "builder" of a *city* —the *"city* of God," the "holy *city"* New Jerusalem.[2] And towers in the Bible—mentioned about 65 times—with the exception of the tower of Babel, were not regarded in a negative way. The Psalmist even referred to the *Lord* as "my high tower" (Ps. 144:2). In another place we read: "The name of the Lord is a strong tower: the righteous runneth into it, and is safe" (Pro. 18:10). If a tower was evil, linking the name of the Lord with it, would be unthinkable.

A tower is no better, or worse, than the purpose for which it is used. There have been churches and ministries that have had a "prayer tower" in which prayer has gone forth around the clock, giving special attention to prayer requests received by phone and letter. This is a good use of a tower!

While it is true that "high places" where idolatrous sacrifices were offered were repeatedly condemned in the Old Testament (2

---

1. Herodotus, *The History,* Book 1:181.   2. Heb. 11:10, Psa. 46:4, Rev. 21:2.

28

Kings 17:11), in other circumstances there were "high places" where valid sacrifices were offered (1 Kings 3:3-5; 1 Sam. 9:12,13). "High" is not necessarily "bad," for even God is often called "The Most High" (Gen. 14:22).

A church for whom I spoke a number of times, believing the steeple on their building was pagan, decided to tear it down. I am not aware that these actions resulted in any special blessing from the Lord; He was already blessing them. I am convinced that He is more concerned about the attitude of the heart, than the slope of a roof. His approval is not based on whether a building has, or does not have, a portion of roof that is so steep it can be called a steeple!

Some have likened church towers to "pillars" or "obelisks." But a vague similarity in architectual style does not establish connection.

It is true that Moses ordered the destruction of idolatrous "pillars" (Deut. 12:3). But not *all* pillars were regarded as evil, for Moses himself, in different circumstances, built twelve "pillars" before which sacrifices were offered to the Lord! (Exod. 24:4). It is the same Hebrew word, *matstsebah,* in each case.[1]

The Lord himself went before Israel as "a *pillar* of a cloud" by day, and "a *pillar* of fire" by night (Exod. 13:21, 22). When his pillar-like presence hovered at the door of the Tabernacle, it became a call to worship (Exod. 33:10). Later, it was a custom for Israelite kings to be crowned as they stood by a "pillar," possibly reminiscent of those days when the presence of the Lord appeared in this form (Judg. 9:6; 2 Kings 11:14).

The Jerusalem Temple featured two large "pillars" in front of it (2 Chron. 3:17) and other pillars also, which Josephus says had

1. *Strong's Concordance,* 4676.

"chapiters made with sculptures after the Corinthian order."[1] When the Psalmist said, "...that our daughters may be as *pillars*, sculptured in palace style" (Psa. 144:12 NKJV), the term was used in a good sense. In the New Testament, those who "overcome" are called "pillars" of the church (Gal. 2:9; Rev. 3:12), and the church itself is called "the *pillar* and ground of the truth" (1 Tim. 3:15).

When I was a boy, the church I attended sponsored a family, making it possible for them to move to the United States to escape the oppression of their native land. Before they learned to speak English, the father would simply point *up*. This was his way of saying he believed in the Lord and was grateful to Him. In somewhat the same way, the inherent significance of a church steeple or spire is that it points heavenward, a majestic symbol of the Christian desire to "seek those things which are *above*" (Col. 3:1). It is not a phallic symbol. It is not a pagan symbol.

A steeple does not identify a police station or prison, an airport or train station, a post office or a school—it does, by common usage, identify a building as a place of Christian worship. This is quite obvious, for when an old church building is sold and used for other purposes, the steeple is removed.

The Bible distinguishes between idolatrous pillars and those that were set up as *monuments*. Rachel's grave was marked with a pillar (Gen. 35:20). Absalom erected a monument, "and called the pillar after his own name" (2 Sam. 18:18). Other pillars were set up to commemorate historical events (Josh. 24:26), and were not regarded as religious objects. The Washington Monument, though built in the shape of an ancient obelisk, is in this category. Its shape, because of its sheer antiquity, carries a certain prestige, long removed from any original pagan meaning. Millions visit it, ride the elevator to the observation deck, and enjoy the bird's-eye view of Washington D.C. from its observation deck. It is not an object of worship.

1. Josephus, *Antiquities of the Jews,* Book 15, 11:5.

30

But there are some who suppose the Washington Monument is a male sex symbol—the largest in the world—standing poised before the capitol dome, a female sex symbol. And, they say, if we add its height (555 feet), plus the length of the base (55.5 feet) and width (55.5 feet), it totals *666!* But this is faulty information.[1]

Some have also sought to promote vulgar meanings regarding the obelisk in front of St. Peter's church in Rome. Because the church faces *east*, at the time of the spring and fall equinox, the rising *sun* causes the shadow of the obelisk (phallus) to penetrate the opening (vagina) in the midst of the "Mother" church, etc. This kind of speculation proves nothing. Both the Tabernacle in the wilderness and the Temple in Jerusalem apparently faced *east*.[2] According to *Harper's Bible Dictionary*, the entrance to the Jerusalem Temple "was so built that at the spring and fall equinoxes sunrise rays entered the Holy of Holies."[3]

If I had within my possession an ancient Egyptian obelisk, would I place it in front of my church? If I were to design a monument, would it be in the shape of an obelisk? No, probably not. But there is no need to make these things out to be worse than they are. I once saw a little tract that said *Nimrod* invented the necktie, the "proof" being that a necktie turned upside down is shaped like an obelisk!

Sometimes a church tower may feature a *bell*, and so we have the terms belfry and bell tower. There is no record of the early Christians using bells, the first *church* bells being mentioned by

1. The actual measurements of the Washington Monument are: 555 feet, 5 1/8th inches tall; each side at the base is 55 feet, 1 1/2 inches *(Worldbook Encyclopedia,* etc.), and so the total is not 666.   2. cf. Exod. 38:13-18; Ezek. 47:1; cf. 8:16.   3. *Harper's Bible Dictionary,* article: "East."

Gregory of Tours about A.D. 585.[1] Bells themselves, however, go back much further—to ancient times—specimens being preserved from various lands, including Babylonia.[2]

Now, by the criteria of some, bells must be pagan: They were not used in the early church; they were known in Babylon where the people worshipped a god named Bel (Jer. 51:44); and, even today, people sing "Jingle Bells" during the Christmas season! But this kind of reasoning can turn someone into a real ding-a-ling!

The Bible itself shows that bells are not bad. Zechariah spoke of "bells" on horses being inscribed with the words: "HOLINESS UNTO THE LORD" (Zech. 14:20). If bells were considered *unholy* objects, these words would certainly be out of place! Even the Lord directed that bells be attached to the hem of the high priest's garment! (Exod. 28:33).

To all of my brothers and sisters in Christ who feel that finding Babylonian origins for present-day customs or practices is of great importance, my advice is to move cautiously in this area, lest we major on minors. If there are things in our lives or churches that are indeed pagan or displeasing to the Lord, they should be dealt with, of course. But in attempting to defuse the confusion of Babylon, we must guard against creating a new "Babylon" of our own making.

1. *The Catholic Encyclopedia*, article: "Bells."   2. Ibid.

Chapter Three

THE MOTHER AND CHILD

Did Nimrod's wife, following his death, give birth to a baby named Tammuz? Did she claim this child was supernaturally conceived and was Nimrod reincarnated? Did this develop into the worship of the Mother and Child that spread to all parts of the world? Did this worship make such an impact that, even today, Roman Catholics still worship Semiramis, even though the name Mary has been substituted? *All* of these things were taught by Hislop!

Hislop says that "from Babylon" the worship of the Mother and Child spread "to the ends of the earth."[1] Whether it was Isis and Osiris in Egypt, or Isi and Iswara in India, or Cybele and Deoius in Asia, or Fortuna and Jupiter in Italy, or Shing Moo with child in China—"the original of that mother, so widely worshipped...was Semiramis," Hislop says, and the original of the child was Tammuz "in his mother's arms."[2]

Hislop implies that the accompanying drawing "from Babylon" —reproduced from Kitto's *Illustrated Commentary*—represents *Semiramis and Tammuz.*[3] But I have carefully scanned literally hundreds of pages of Kitto's writings and have found no confirmation for this whatsoever!

1. Hislop, pp. 20, 21.   2. Ibid.   3. Ibid., p. 19.

33

Multiplied millions of women have given birth to a baby! Why should we suppose that only *one* of these mothers—Semiramis —was copied as an object of worship? Primitive people, with good reason, regarded the birth of a baby with a distinct awe. It would have been a natural development for them to worship images of a mother and child. But this does not seem to occur to Hislop.

To Hislop, even a similarity that is very general in nature, is considered a connecting link. "Ceres...is the same as the great goddess of Babylon," he reasons, *"for* Ceres was worshipped with the babe at her breast, even as the Babylonian goddess was."[1] Finding similarities in the way artists have portrayed Mary with the infant Jesus—the accompanying drawing for example—Hislop supposes that Roman Catholics today still worship *Semiramis!*

In making this point, Hislop even appeals to the color of Mary's hair in some paintings from centuries past. Until "Raphael somewhat departed from the beaten track," he says, "the Madonna was *always* represented with blue eyes and golden hair."[2] He supposes this was because artists were copying the hair color of Semiramis. But would a Babylonian woman have blond hair and blue eyes?

As usual, Hislop's examples are disjointed. He cites references from various poets and writers who mentioned the "yellow-haired Ceres"; "the yellow-haired Europa," whom Jupiter carried away in the form of a bull; Diana, the huntress, "the yellow-haired daughter of Jupiter"; Dione, the mother of Venus, called "yellow-haired"; "the yellow-haired" Minerva; the "golden ringlets" of the snake-haired gorgon Medusa; and the "golden hair" of Ariadne, the wife of Bacchus.[3] But considering that thousands of "goddesses" have been worshipped, it is no feat to produce a list of several who had golden hair.

---

1. Hislop, p. 76. 2. Ibid., p. 85. 3. Ibid., p.85, 86.

34

Finally, attempting to link golden hair with Semiramis, Hislop mentions Atergatis who, in mythology, was Semiramis' mother or possibly Semiramis herself, a Syrian *fish-goddess*. He then passes over many centuries—and to an entirely different part of the world—to "The Ellewoman," a Scandinavian mermaid, mentioned in the fairy tales of Hans Christian Andersen! She is described as "sitting on the surface of the waters, and combing her long golden hair with a golden comb"![1]

As strained as all of this is, Hislop concludes: "When, therefore, it is known that the most famed pictures of the Virgin Mother in Italy represented her as of a fair complexion and with golden hair...who can resist the conclusion that she must have been thus represented, only because she had been copied from the same prototype [Semiramis] as the Pagan divinities?"[2]

"It is this very goddess that is now worshipped in the Church of Rome under the name of Mary," Hislop says. "Though that goddess is called by the name of the mother of our Lord, *all the attributes* given to her are derived simply from the Babylonian Madonna, and not from the Virgin Mother of Christ."[3]

But every single Roman Catholic I have ever known has regarded Mary as a woman of spotless character, a virgin, one that was totally dedicated to God and virtue—not any of these attributes fit Semiramis! Her lifestyle was the very opposite!

According to the legends, Semiramis first married Prince Omnes. When she left him to marry Ninus, he committed suicide. She took handsome soldiers to bed, after which she had them killed. Across western Asia there are mounds of Semiramis, said to be graves of the one night lovers she buried alive![4] Hislop's own writings describe her as "the incarnation of *every kind of licentiousness*"[5] and that "the licentious and dissolute life of Semiramis gave her *many children.*"[6]

According to Roman Catholic doctrine, Mary gave birth to only *one* child—Jesus Christ—and remained a virgin throughout her life. To say, then, that the immoral Semiramis, the mother of

1. Hislop, p. 86.   2. Ibid.   3. Ibid., p. 265.   4. Monaghan, *Goddesses and Heroines.*
5. Hislop, p. 88.   6. Ibid., p. 69.

35

"many children," is "the very goddess that is now worshipped in the Church of Rome under the name of Mary" is simply not a feasible conclusion!

Because Hislop claims the doctrines of the Roman Catholic Church "in all essential respects, have been derived from Babylon,"[1] it would bolster his claim if he could show that Semiramis was worshipped as a *virgin*. But in view of her immoral lifestyle, if the Babylonians believed this, they were really crazy!

Referring to the Biblical prophecy that "a virgin shall conceive, and bear a son" (Isa. 7:14), Hislop says: "Isaiah's prophecy was carried by the Jewish captives to Babylon, and hence the *new* [italics are his] title bestowed upon the Babylonian goddess."[2] If this was a "new" title for the Babylonian goddess, at the time of the captivity, then she was *not* worshipped as a virgin back at the time of Nimrod or the intervening centuries!

Among the multiplied millions of people referred to as "pagans," did some worship virgin goddesses? Doubtless they did—and goddesses that were *not* virgins. With thousands of years of history, and vast numbers of diverse peoples, one might cite examples of all kinds of goddesses that were worshipped!

Did the fact that various ancient religions had mother goddesses contribute to the exaltation of Mary within the Roman Catholic Church? Apparently there were some who felt Christianity lacked a mother figure of high status and eventually began to look to Mary in this capacity. In time, this concept grew into the elaborate doctrine so widely held today. But this was no part of the original faith. As *The Encyclopedia Britannica* states, during the first centuries of the Church, no emphasis was placed upon Mary whatsoever.[3]

According to the Scriptures, Mary was a devout woman who conceived as a virgin, being supernaturally overshadowed by the Holy Spirit. She was blessed among women to be the mother of our Savior, but she was not a savior herself (Lk. 1:42, 47). We believe the devotion of Roman Catholics to Mary has gone beyond what

1. Hislop, p. 129.   2. Ibib., p. 76.   3. *Encyclopedia Britannica*, article: "Mary."

36

the Scriptures justify, but this does not prove they worship Nimrod's wife Semiramis!

Another wild claim of Hislop is that the Roman Catholic practice of priestly celibacy was started by Semiramis! Though she was grossly immoral, and "the Mysteries over which she presided were scenes of the rankest pollution," he claims that "the higher orders of the priesthood were bound to a life of celibacy....The voice of antiquity assigns to that abandoned queen the invention of clerical celibacy, and that in the most stringent form."[1]

The "stringent form" to which Hislop refers is *castration*. But his authority for this, Ammianus Marcellinus, says nothing about the castration of *priests*. He speaks, rather, of the disgusting state of eunuch slaves, "sallow and disfigured...so that, wherever anyone goes, beholding the troops of mutilated men, he would curse the memory of that Queen Semiramis of old, who was the first of all to castrate young males, thus doing violence, as it were, to Nature."[2] An editor's note says: "That she was the originator of castration is not found elsewhere." But if the obscure reference is correct, there is still nothing that would imply Semiramis castrated young males to make them priests!

Hislop can only assume this by making Semiramis the same as Cybele. Then he says: "Every scholar knows that when the worship of Cybele, the Babylonian [?] goddess, was introduced into Pagan Rome, it was introduced in its primitive form, with its celibate clergy."[3] If one looks up the reference for this statement, he will read the following fable related by Pausanias:

> Zeus in his sleep let fall seed on the ground, and...the earth produced a demon with two genital organs, one of a man and one of a woman; and this demon they named Agdistis. But the gods...cut off his male organ....From it sprang an almond tree...a daughter of the river Sangarius took of the fruit and put it in her bosom...and she conceived. The male child whom she bore [Attis]...grew in stature...and Agdistis loved him. But...his relations sent him to Pessinus to wed the king's daughter. As the wedding song was being sung, Agdistis appeared, and Attis in a fit of madness *mutilated himself.*[4]

1. Hislop, p. 219.   2. Ammianus Marcellinus, *Roman History*, Book 14:6.   3. Hislop, p. 220.   4. Pausanias, *Pausanias' Description of Greece*, Book 7:17.

37

It is said that the priests of Cybele, called Corybantes and Galli, were emasculated to commemorate the emasculation of Attis, the beloved of Cybele. To achieve unity with the goddess, they dressed like women and celebrated her festivals with wild dances and orgiastic excesses.[1]

It was "from the *very same source*," says Hislop, speaking of the priests of Cybele, that the Pope "introduced into the priesthood under his authority the binding obligation of celibacy."[2] But this does not fit. Roman Catholic priests are not castrated. They are not dressed like women. And the *time* when celibacy developed within the Roman Catholic Church, is far removed—by many centuries —from the period when the worship of Cybele was in vogue. Where is the connection? Better arguments against priestly celibacy are found within the Bible itself (1 Tim. 3:2; 4:3).

While there have been Roman Catholic priests who have fallen into immorality, many have taken their vows seriously—have set aside marriage and having a family of their own—in order to comply with the teachings of their church. To suppose they did this because Nimrod's wife, Semiramis, was worshipped by some castrated priests, is really farfetched. Has there ever been even *one* Roman Catholic priest who did it for this reason?

"WEEPING FOR TAMMUZ"

According to Hislop, Semiramis gave birth to Tammuz, mentioned by name in one Biblical reference: "...women weeping for Tammuz" (Ezek. 8:14). Finding examples of other gods at various times and places for whom people *wept*—such as the god Balder in Iceland or Bacchus in Greece—Hislop assumes all of these must have been originally Tammuz![3] It does not seem to occur to him that weeping for someone who died, was a natural development, not requiring a common original.

Nevertheless, by evidence no stronger than this, Hislop supposes that numerous ancient deities were all Tammuz! He says that Tammuz was "Baal-berith, Lord of the Covenant," mentioned in Judges 8:33, his proof being no more than a drawing of a winged

1. *New Century Classical Handbook*, p. 345.   2. Hislop, p. 220.   3. Ibid., p. 57.

child-god sitting on a rainbow, to which he adds this comment: "In this character he is represented in Persian monuments as seated on the rainbow, the well-known symbol of the covenant."[1]

Cupid, the love god, is sometimes pictured with bow and arrows, and so Hislop takes this to mean Cupid was Tammuz. "To identify this infant divinity, with his father 'the mighty hunter,' he was equipped with 'bow and arrows'."[2]

As Hislop merges myths together, Tammuz is made into all the following:

Adonis. "Tammuz was called...Adonis" (p. 70).

Alorus. "The name Tammuz...was equivalent to Alorus or the god of fire" (p. 245).

Cupid. "The boy-god...Cupid...his father the mighty hunter" (p. 189).

Fire. "Fire itself was worshipped as Tammuz" (p. 315).

Hercules. "Hercules, one form of the Pagan Messiah..." (p. 112).

Horus. "The Babylonians...worshipped...an infant or child in his mother's arms...Horus" (p. 20).

Iswara. "The Child...worshipped...in India" (p. 20).

Janus. "Tammuz or Janus, in his character as...the woman's seed, was just an incarnation [of Satan]" (p. 279).

Jupiter. "The Mother and Child were worshipped...as Fortuna and Jupiter-puer, or Jupiter, the boy" (p. 20).

1. Hislop, p. 70.   2. Ibid., p. 189.

39

Mithras. "Tammuz was called...Mithras" (p. 70).

Nimrod. "Tammuz was Nimrod....Nimrod was Tammuz" (pp. 314, 315).

Ninus. "Ninus...the son of Semiramis" (p. 22).

Plutus. "The Mother and Child [were worshipped] as Irene ...with the boy Plutus in her arms" (p. 20).

Oannes. "Tammuz or Nimrod was called...Oannes" (p. 114).

Osiris. "Osiris...identical with Tammuz" (p. 56).

Sun-divinity. "Tammuz was the Sun-divinity" (p. 118).

Vishnu. "Tammuz was called...Vishnu, the Preserver or Savior of men" (p. 70).

Vejovis. "Vejovis—that is 'Young Jupiter' [in the arms of the goddess]" (p. 140).

Zoroaster. "Tammuz was...the same as Zoroaster, the god of the ancient fire-worshippers" (p. 121).

Myth mixing does have its problems, for if these various ones were all Tammuz, then he was killed by a wild boar,[1] was slain by the treachery of the god Loki,[2] was torn in pieces by dogs,[3] the tower of Babel fell on him,[4] he was killed and cut in pieces by Typhon or the Teitans.[5] But, Hislop concludes, "Shem was the *actual* slayer of Tammuz"![6]

What could possibly be the basis for saying *Shem,* Noah's son, killed Tammuz? In mythology, Hercules fought in defence of Heaven and killed the rebel giants, which Hislop supposes included Nimrod (Tammuz). But who was Hercules? Hislop says, "If Shem was at that time alive, as beyond question he was, who so likely as he? In exact accordance with this deduction, we find that one of the names of the primitive Hercules in Egypt was 'Sem'."[7] His authority for this statement—Wilkinson—says: "The Hercules of Egypt was called Gom...or, according to some, Chon, Gignon, Gigon, or *Sem.*"[8] But Wilkinson says nothing about Hercules (or Sem) being Shem, the son of Noah. Hislop, ignoring the context of this reference, builds only on a similarity in names.

---

1. Hislop, p. 100   2. Ibid., p. 57.   3. Ibid., p.22.   4. Ibid., p.55.   5. Ibid., p. 276.
6. Ibid.   7. Ibid., p. 63.   8. Wilkinson, *The Ancient Egyptians,* vol. 5, p. 17.

Shem, Noah's son, was an actual person. It would seem from reading Hislop that Tammuz was also an actual person—"a person of great stature and immense bodily powers, as well as most fascinating manners"[1]—one who could be actually killed by Shem. But in checking the various encyclopedias, Tammuz is *never* described as an actual person; he is *never* mentioned as the son of Nimrod; Semiramis is *never* mentioned as his mother! *These are all inventions of Hislop!*

Tammuz was regarded as a food and vegetation god; a power in the sap that rises in the date palm and its fruit; a power in plants, grain, beer, and milk. Each year when the heat of summer had caused vegetation to wither and die, primitive people took this as a sign their vegetation gods, such as Tammuz, had "died." Annually, women—representing the bereaved mother, sister, and young widow of Tammuz—would weep for him in the month that is still called Tammuz in the Jewish calendar (our late June and early July).[2]

Because June 24—St. John's Day—is at this time of year, Hislop says this date was chosen by the Roman Catholic Church to perpetuate the worship of Tammuz![3] He labors to show that Oannes, who came forth from the sea as a fish-god, is but another name for Tammuz.[4] Having thus set the stage, he presents his major argument: in the Latin language of the Roman Church, the name John was *Joannes*, obviously similar in spelling to *Oannes*! "To make the festival of the 24th of June, then, suit Christians and Pagans alike, all that was needful was just to call it the festival of Joannes; and thus the Christians would suppose that they were honoring John the Baptist, while the Pagans were still worshipping their old god Oannes, or Tammuz."[5]

But this does not fit. Hislop says that "the name Oannes could be known only to the initiated."[6] If so, June 24 could not have been a *widely popular* day by this name. How, then, could there be any advantage gained by turning "Oannes' Day" into "Joannes' Day"?

John baptized with "water." Oannes rose up out of "water." For some, I suppose, this may seem like a connecting link. But

1. Hislop, p. 21. 2. *Theological Wordbook of the Old Testament,* vol. 2, p. 972. 3. Ibid., p. 113, 114. 4. Ibid., p. 114. 5. Ibid. 6. Ibid., p. 121.

how? The water John baptized in was the Jordan River; the water from which Oannes rose was the Persian Gulf! John was a real person; Oannes, an imaginary fish-god! Where is there any possible connection?

The birth of John the Baptist occurred six months before that of Jesus (Lk. 2:36). If one wants to argue that the dates of December 25 and, consequently, June 24 are incorrect as birth dates for Jesus and John, this is one thing. It is another thing to claim that Roman Catholics deliberately sought to perpetuate the worship of Tammuz, to deceive Christians, by subtly substituting the name of John the Baptist!

Having said that St. John's Day is really Tammuz Day, Hislop comes up with another novel idea about Tammuz—that St. Swithin (though generally believed to have been Bishop of Winchester in the ninth century) was none other than Tammuz! He mentions a superstition regarding St. Swithin's Day—that if it rains on this day, it will rain for six weeks. Because six weeks is 40 days rounded off, he reasons that "the patron saint of the forty days' rain was just Tammuz...*as the incarnation of Noah,* in whose time it rained forty days and forty nights without intermission. Tammuz and St. Swithin, *then,* must have been *one and the same*"![1]

As ridiculous as this is, Hislop goes further. "Long before the Christian era, Tammuz had come to be recognized as an incarnation of the Devil," and so, because "St. Swithin is no other than St. Satan," the Papacy actually canonized *Satan!*[2]

According to Hislop, Roman Catholic leaders also canonized Bacchus (who he identifies with Nimrod)! At earlier times they would not have been able to get away with this, he explains, but by the time of the Dark Ages, they "had the unblushing effrontery to give the grand Pagan adversary of the Son of God" *sainthood,* calling him "St. Bacchus the Martyr"![3] His feast day is designated as October 7. This date follows soon after the end of vintage—when some cultures celebrated with wine drinking—and so, *on this basis,* Hislop argues: "This 'St. Bacchus the Martyr' was the identical Bacchus of the Pagans, the god of drunkenness and debauchery"![4]

1. Hislop, p. 280.   2. Ibid., pp. 280, 281.   3. Ibid., p. 121, 122.   4. Ibid. .

But *The Catholic Encyclopedia* tells it differently: Bacchus the Martyr died in the Diocletian persecution in about 303 A.D. His martyrdom is well authenticated by the earliest martyrologies and historians like Theodoret. It is said he was examined under torture and beaten so severely with thongs that he died under the blows. The feast day for Bacchus the Martyr, along with some others, is October 7.[1]

According to the Hislop scenario, something like the following would have occurred. When a group of Roman Catholic leaders assembled, someone suggested:

"Why don't we do something really bizarre, like granting 'sainthood' to someone especially evil—someone like the old drunken god Bacchus?"

"But how can we pull this off?" one of them questioned. "Someone might catch on to our scheme."

"I know what we can do," another answered. "We can make up a story about a man who would not deny his faith in Christ, and was so severely beaten that he died. We'll call him 'St. Bacchus the Martyr'! In time a lot of gullible Christians will believe our story, unaware that we have really set up the pagan god Bacchus as a saint!"

To us, this explanation lacks feasibility and connection. What purpose would it serve, one way or the other? It is very possible there was indeed a Christian martyr who happened to have the name Bacchus. A Christian woman may have the name Diana— this does not make her the *goddess* Diana! The Christian preacher Apollos (Acts 18:24) was not the pagan god Apollo. Nor was the Christian by the name of Narcissus (Rom. 16:11) the same as the youth by this name in mythology.

Yet, based on nothing more than this—a similarity in name—Hislop supposes St. *Satur* is the pagan god *Saturn*! "The name by which Nimrod was known as the god of the Chaldean Mysteries...was *Saturn*," he says, and the Roman Catholic Church has canonized him as *"St. Satur"*![2] He goes on to say that "Mystery" signifies a hidden system, so Nimrod or Saturn, as the god of the Chaldean

1. *The Catholic Encyclopedia*, article: "Sergius and Bacchus."   2. Hislop, p. 269.

Mysteries, signifies *the Hidden God*. Having given us this "definition," he cites the words of an obscure Roman Catholic prayer:

"GOD HIDDEN, and my Savior, have mercy upon us."

Then he asks: "Whence can this invocation of the 'God Hidden' have come, but from the ancient worship of Saturn, the 'Hidden God'?"[1] Our answer is: It is far more likely this wording came from the *Bible!* "Verily thou art a God that HIDEST thyself, O God of Israel, the SAVIOR" (Isa. 45:15).

Hislop commonly bases claims on a mere similarity in spelling —Joannes/Oannes, Satur/Saturn, and Kamut/gamut. He says that Kamut is but another name for Nimrod or Osiris, and,

> when Gregory the Great introduced into the Church of Rome what are now called the Gregorian Chants; he...introduced the music of *Kamut*"; and so the name of "*Kamut*...is in every-day use among ourselves as the name of the musical scale; for what is the melody...consisting of the 'seven vowels' formed into a hymn, but—the *Gamut?*[2]

Dictionaries define "gamut" as the whole series of musical notes, and, in the broad sense, an entire range or series. But we have yet to find any evidence that would link "gamut" with Kamut!

Such claims, when not totally ridiculous, are at best questionable. According to Hislop, by changing one letter, Baal-berith, "Lord of the Covenant," becomes Baal-bereth, signifying "Lord of the fir-tree," supposedly linking Christmas trees with Baal worship![3] He attempts to link the word Easter with Ishtar, but Ishtar means "star," as does Esther,[4] mentioned in the Bible, and is not the same as the word Easter. "Easter" and "Astarte" have the same letters—as do the words "Santa" and "Satan"— but what does it prove? True doctrinal beliefs cannot be built on a mere similarity of letters. By this method, one could say the "Epistles" were the wives of the "Apostles." Or imagine someone teaching: "Don't say 'Hello'—it sounds like Hell!"

Pointing out that it was a custom for priests, of various kinds, to eat of the sacrifices they offered, Hislop says: "Hence, the

---

1. Hislop, p. 269. 2. Ibid., p. 22, 23. 3. Ibid., p. 98. 4. *Hastings' Dictionary of the Bible*, article: "Esther."

44

priests of Nimrod or Baal were necessarily required to eat of the human sacrifices; and thus it has come to pass that 'Cahna-Bal,' the 'Priest of Baal,' is the established word in our own tongue for a devourer of human flesh."[1] But check *any* etymological dictionary —none will support this supposition. Instead, "cannibal," dating from about 1553, comes from the name of the inhabitants of the Carib Islands—the Caribales or Canibales—who were reported to be man-eaters.[2]

Equally questionable are the following: "Nimrod" signifies "the subduer of the leopard," from *Nimr*, a "leopard," and *rad* "to subdue";[3] Shinar (Gen. 11:2), the land of Nimrod, comes from *shene*, "to repeat," and *naar*, "childhood," meaning the land of the "Regenerator";[4] the name of Nimrod's (supposed) son, Tammuz, is derived from *tam*, "to make perfect," and *muz*, "fire," meaning "Fire the perfecter";[5] and the meaning of the name Cush, Nimrod's father, is "The numberer" or "Arithmetician."[6]

Hislop claims to find Cush in all kinds of names: Chaos or Chus;[7] Cuth or Cuath;[8] Chusorus, Khesha, Khesa;[9] Bac-chus;[10] Nar-kissos;[11] and even in the name Zernebogus, a black ill-omened divinity![12]

By dividing this name as Zer-Nebo-Gus, Hislop supposes it means "The seed of the prophet Cush," i.e. Nimrod![13] This is like dividing "television" into Te-Levi-Sion, as some have done, providing the basis for a senseless teaching about *Te* (the symbol for *tellurium*, a chemical element), the tribe of *Levi*, and that area of Jerusalem called *Sion*![14] By this method, one could say that Tam-muz invented the Tam-bourine (its round shape being in honor of the sun-god, of course) or that the name Hislop means His-slop!

In somewhat the same way, years ago a prophecy preacher who supposed Mussolini was the Antichrist, took the phrase "noise of thy *viols*" (Isa. 14:11) as a reference to Mussolini's *violin* playing!

1. Hislop, p. 232.   2. *The Encyclopedia Americana,* article: "Cannibalism."   3. Hislop. p. 44.   4. Ibid., p. 137.   5. Ibid., p. 245.   6. Ibid., p. 95, 245.   7. Ibid., p. 27.   8. Ibid., p. 49.   9. Ibid., p. 50.   10. Ibid., p. 48, 49.   11. Ibid., p. 156.   12. Ibid., pp. 33, 34.   13. Ibid.   14. In reality, "television" is made up of two words: *tele* (far) and *vision* (to view), and so viewing from afar.

If we allow this kind of word manipulation, one could make all kinds of silly claims:

Rebekah smoked cigarettes, for she "lighted off the camel" (Gen. 24:64).

People with swimming pools beware; there shall be "earthquakes in divers places" (Matt. 24:7).

The term "the abomination of desolation" means "the A-bomb of desolation" (Matt. 24:15).

Gog, the intruder coming into Israel to take a "spoil," must really be coming for "oil" (Ezek. 38:13).

"Gog," ironically, must be the Jews, for the word appears in "synaGOGue of Satan" (Rev. 3:9).

There must be a hidden meaning in the letters USA appearing in the word JerUSAlem.

One should be careful not to base too much on *parts* of words. "Africa" and "America" each end with the letters *rica,* but this does not make them the same place.

People from Armenia commonly have names ending with the letters *ian.* (I have known people with names like Shakarian, Deukmejian, Krekorian, Erysian, etc.) One might conclude, therefore, that words ending with *ian* have an Armenian origin. But *many* words end in *ian*: Babylonian, Egyptian, Persian, Ethiopian, Corinthian, Galatian, Ephesian, Jordanian, Russian, Brazilian, Indian, Hawaiian, Canadian, Episcopalian, Presbyterian, and even Christian—to mention a few!

True etymology is based on more than a similarity in sound or spelling, as may be seen in the following: Do people in Turkey eat a lot of turkey and those in Greece eat grease? Do people in Jamaica eat jam? Are people in Hungary hungry? Have people been gypped who live in Egypt? Is a Roman one who roams? Are Russians always in a rush? If I ran in a race, am I from Iran? Are people on the island of Haiti filled with hate and those on Madagascar mad? Was the can invented in Canada? Was the cube invented in Cuba and poles in Poland? Did pans originate in Panama, or Japan? Did ants come from Antarctica and many germs from Germany?

46

Hislop manipulates words around until he even links the word "Nun" with Nimrod! He says Nimrod was the same as Ninus; that Ninus in Chaldee can be either Nin or Non, meaning son; the feminine of Non is Nonna, meaning daughter—"just the Popish canonical name for a Nun."[1]

Hislop also taught that a synonym of Nin was Nor—that "however strange it may seem to the English reader, the Hebrew o was often pronounced as hard g. 'Nor'...is also Ngr. What if this be the origin of the well-known word Nigger or Negro? Tribes were often called by the name of the god they worshipped,"[2] and so, supposedly, another reference to Nimrod!

Attempting to reinforce his position that Nimrod was a Negro, and that all the worship of the Mother and Child in the world —including India—spread from Babylon, Hislop gives the accompanying drawing which he describes in these words: "In India, the infant Crishna (emphatically the *black* god), in the arms of the goddess Devaki, is represented with the wooly hair and marked features of the Negro."[3]

It has been said that a "communicator" takes the complex and makes it simple; a "complicator" takes the simple and makes it complex. It seems to us that trying to base arguments about errors in the Roman Catholic Church (or any other group) on details about Nimrod and Semiramis tends to complicate and confuse, rather than clarify the real issues involved.

1. Hislop, p. 223.   2. Quoted in "The Saturday Review," September 17, 1859.   3. Hislop, p. 238.

47

Chapter Four

"MYSTERY BABYLON"

In the book of Revelation, John describes a woman "arrayed in purple and scarlet color, and decked with gold and precious stones and pearls, having a golden cup in her hand full of abominations." On her forehead she has a name: "MYSTERY, BABYLON THE GREAT, THE MOTHER OF HARLOTS AND ABOMINATIONS OF THE EARTH" (Rev. 17:4, 5). According to Hislop, this symbolic woman called "Mystery Babylon" pictures the Roman Catholic Church. Many of us have held this position, but if we look at the evidence point by point, it may not be as solid as we supposed.

"Mystery Babylon" is described as holding a *cup* in her hand (Rev. 17:4). Hislop tries to tie this in with Semiramis and the accompanying drawing titled: "Woman with cup from Babylon."[1] But this hardly fits, for his footnote on the very same page, citing Pliny, refers to "the cup of Semiramis" as weighing 1,200 pounds! Hislop explains that this drawing was reproduced from Kitto's *Biblical Cyclopedia.* But when we check this  source, Kitto says nothing about this women with a cup being Semiramis—only that this drawing gives some idea of the *clothing* worn by the Babylonians.[2]

Nevertheless, Hislop says Semiramis, the Chaldean queen, was a remarkable type of the harlot with a cup in her hand called

1. Hislop, p. 5.   2. Kitto, *Biblical Cyclopedia,* article: "Babylon."

 "Mystery Babylon." He then gives the accompanying drawing—a medal struck by Pope Leo XII in 1825—described in these words: "The Church of Rome symbolized as a 'Woman,' holding in her left hand a cross, and in her right a CUP."[1] But where is the connection? The cups in the two drawings are not even the same shape! The cup shown here was clearly intended to represent a cup used for communion. If the Roman Catholic Church is "Mystery Babylon," the evidence needs to be based on more than two disconnected and unrelated drawings of a woman holding a cup!

A cup, in itself, is not an evil symbol, for also in the book of Revelation, the Lord is pictured as holding a *cup!* (Rev. 14:10, 16:19). "In the hand of the Lord there is a *cup*..." (Psalms 75:8). A *cup* is even used as a symbol of salvation! (Ps. 116:13). In the New Testament, "cup" is used as a verbal symbol, representative of Christ's shed blood: "The *cup* of blessing which we bless, is it not the communion of the blood of Christ?" (1 Cor. 10:16).

The harlot called "Mystery Babylon" is "arrayed in *purple* and *scarlet* color" (Rev. 17:4). There is a tendency for some to immediately link these colors with the bright and highly decorated vestments worn by the Pope and others within the hierarchy of the Roman Catholic Church. But, again these colors provide no conclusive identification.

Purple and scarlet were used for the Tabernacle curtains (Exod. 26:1), the veil of the Temple (2 Chron. 3:14), and garments worn by the Old Testament priests (Exod. 28:6,8,15). An early Christian convert, Lydia, was a seller of purple (Acts 16:14). Proverbs mentions the family of the "virtuous woman" as being clothed in scarlet (Prov. 31:21). Daniel—certainly not a compromiser with worldly ways—was honored by being clothed in scarlet (Dan. 5:29).

The harlot of Revelation 17 is called *"Mystery* Babylon," which Hislop links with the long-held practice of conducting Roman Catholic services in Latin. Because most people could not understand

1 Hislop, p. 6.

what was being said—it was like a "mystery" to them. Having pointed this out, Hislop goes on to say:

> When, therefore, the Pope calls his Church the *Latin* Church, that is equivalent to a declaration that it is the Church of 'Mystery.' Thus, by this very name of the Pope's own choosing, he has with his own hands written upon the very forehead of his apostate communion its divine Apocalyptic designation, MYSTERY—Babylon the great.[1]

It should be plain to see, however, this argument is not very strong, for the Bible itself uses phrases such as:

> "The wisdom of God in a *mystery*" (1 Cor. 2:7), "the *mystery* of Christ" (Eph. 3:4), "a great *mystery*...concerning Christ and the church" (Eph. 5:32), the *"mystery"* of "Christ in you, the hope of glory" (Col. 1:27), "the *mystery* of the gospel" (Eph. 6:19), "the fellowship of the *mystery*" (Eph. 3:9), "the *mystery* of the faith" (1 Tim. 3:9), and the *"mystery* of godliness" (1 Tim. 3:16)!

"Mystery Babylon" is described as seated on *"seven mountains"* (Rev. 17:9). Hislop says: "To call Rome the city 'of the seven hills' was by its citizens held to be as descriptive as to call it by its own proper name," and so, "the Church which has its seat and headquarters on the seven hills of Rome might most appropriately be called 'Babylon'."[2] In another place, he describes the Pope as "he who has his seat on the seven hills of Rome."[3]

But it is the *Vatican* Hill that is the seat of the Pope and the headquarters of the Roman Catholic Church—*this was not one of the seven hills of Rome!* This district "did not belong to ancient Rome, nor was it included within the city walls built by Emperor Aurelian."[4] *Harper's Bible Dictionary* includes a map confirming this point.[5]

The seven hills on which Rome was built are these: the Palatine Hill, the Capitoline Hill, the Quirinal Hill, the Aventine Hill, the Caelian Hill, the Esquiline Hill, and the Viminal Hill. The Vatican Hill, across the Tiber to the west, is not one of the seven.

1. Hislop, p. 271.   2. Ibid., pp. 1, 2 (Introduction).   3. Ibid., p. 271.   4. *The Catholic Encyclopedia,* article: "Vatican."   5. *Harper's Bible Dictionary,* article: "Rome."

It should be pointed out, also, that the term the prophecy actually uses is "seven *mountains.*" The seven hills of Rome would hardly qualify as mountains, all of which have minimal elevations. The *highest* is Quirinal Hill—a mere 226 above sea level! St. Peter's church itself—*just the building*—is nearly double this! I can speak first hand about its height, having climbed the stairway between the inner and outer casing of the dome, all the way up in 1978. It is 434 feet from the floor to the cross on top.

Attempting to show the *immoral* status of Rome, Hislop says, "In 1836 the whole number of births in Rome was 4,373, while of these *no fewer than 3,160 were foundlings!*"[1] (Foundlings are infants found after their unknown parents have abandoned them.) This was so long ago, it would be difficult now to obtain exact information, but these numbers do not seem feasible to me.

On the subject of the book of Revelation, it is probably needless to say there are different schools of thought! But Hislop comes up with some strange views of his own. Concerning Revelation 12:9—"And the great dragon was cast out, that old serpent called the Devil, and Satan, which deceiveth the whole world: he was cast out into the earth, and his angels were cast out with him"—Hislop says this was fulfilled in the 4th century when "Gratian abolished the legal provision for the support of the fire-worship and serpent-worship of Rome."[2]

A few verses later in Revelation 12, we read that "the serpent cast out of his mouth a flood of *water* after the woman" who fled into the wilderness (Rev. 12:15). So intent on discrediting the doctrine of baptismal regeneration, Hislop says: "The water cast out of the mouth of the serpent *must be the water of baptismal regeneration*"![3] I am not aware of even *one* Biblical expositor, of *any* denominational background, who holds this view!

Regarding the prophetic time period of 1,260 days (Rev. 12:6; 13:5), Hislop says "the Pope of Rome was made Universal Bishop" in A.D. 606, and "it is from this period only that the well-known 1,260 days can begin to be counted."[4] Using the year-for-a-day method, he then projected 1866 as the end of the 1,260 days (years),

1. Hislop, p. 220.   2. Ibid., p.280.   3. Ibid., p. 247.   4. Ibid., p. 255.

a date he did not live to see. Just what he thought would happen is not clear. If he believed this would be the year of the Lord's Second Advent, he stopped short of saying so. Perhaps he had learned a lesson from the Adventists' "Great Disappointment" of 1844, which would have been only a few years before he wrote.

As to the "image of the Beast" (Rev. 13:14), Hislop says this is the image of the Virgin Mary as worshipped by Roman Catholics! The "Mary" they worship, he claims, is none other than Nimrod's wife, Semiramis, who came to be known by the name "Semelé, which, in the Babylonian language, signifies THE IMAGE"![1]

6 6 6

Regarding the *"number* of the Beast...the number of a *man"*—666—it is no surprise that Hislop attempts to take it back to a man in Babylon. You guessed it! *Nimrod.* But before looking at this, we will consider some other explanations that have been offered.

Because the number 666—the number of a name—can be *counted* (Rev. 13:17, 18), it is presumably a name in a language such as Hebrew, Greek, or Latin in which letters have a numerical value. Using Hebrew letters, some commentators have zeroed in on Nero Caesar, either as the actual person, or a type of the one who would ultimately fulfill the prophecy. Written in Hebrew as NRON KSR, we have:

N	R	O	N	K	S	R		
50	200	6	50	100	60	200	=	666.

Early on, Irenaeus (c. A.D. 130—c. 202) suggested the name TEITAN, the Greek letters of which total 666:

T	E	I	T	A	N		
300	5	10	300	1	50	=	666.

Also, though he considered it less probable, Irenaeus mentioned LATEINOS, meaning the Latin kingdom, as counting up to 666. He warned, however, against speculation, "inasmuch as many names can be found possessing the number mentioned."[2]

1. Hislop, pp. 264, 265. 2. Irenaeus, *Against Heresies,* v. 30.3.

Andreas Helwig (c. 1572-1643) was probably the first to obtain 666 from the title VICARIUS FILII DEI (Vicar of the Son of God).[1] The Latin letters of this title that have a numerical value are these:

V I C A R I V S   F I L I I   D E I
5 1 100   1 5   1 50 1 1   500   1 = 666

For many years it was commonly believed among Seventh-day Adventists (and others) that the words "Vicarius Filii Dei" are inscribed on a crown worn by the Pope. This was based on an article in a Catholic publication, *Our Sunday Visitor,* April 18, 1915, which evidently contained faulty information.[2] Consequently, *The Seventh-day Adventist Commentary*, while no longer claiming that the title appears on the Pope's crown, does favor "Vicarius Filii Dei" as the best explanation regarding 666.[3]

In time, what would be a strange twist, however, was the discovery that the name of the prophetess of the Seventh-day Adventist church, ELLEN GOULD WHITE, also contains the number 666! Bearing in mind that in Latin a U is written as a V, and allowing that a W (double U is a double V), we have:

E L L E N   G O V L D   V V H I T E
50 50   5 50 500   5 5   1   = 666

When the administration of President Franklin Delano Roosevelt required people to receive a Social Security number, some wondered if this might be the mark of the Beast. Was his popularity allowing him to appear "as a lamb" while he might really be a "dragon"? (cf. Rev. 13:11). Was he "making fire come down from heaven" by using electricity to transmit his "fireside" chats on radio? (cf. Rev. 13:13). It took some manipulation, but by using the spelling of the family name in Holland—Van Rosenvelvt—the letters that are Roman numerals could be made to total 666!

Obviously, *many* names, can be made to count up to 666! If a name does not work in one language, another can be tried, use a different spelling, or add a title! By such methods, as *The Pulpit*

---

1. Froom, *The Prophetic Faith of Our Fathers,* vol. 2, pp. 605-608.   2. This has been acknowledged, in response to a letter I wrote, in a Catholic publication, "The Wanderer" (August 4, 1994), which also points out that the *official* papal title is *Vicarius Christi,* not *Vicarius Filii Dei.*   3. *The Seventh-day Adventist Commentary,* vol. 7, pp. 823, 824.

Commentary points out, 666 can be obtained from names like Caligula, Trajan, Julian the Apostate, Benedict IX, Paul V, Mohammed, Martin Luther, John Calvin, Napoleon, and others.[1]

Hislop, joining the club, feels *his* explanation is "beyond all possibility of doubt"![2] He tells us that Nimrod, as the god of the Chaldean Mysteries, was known as Saturn, which, "as every Chaldee scholar knows," is spelled with four letters, *Stur*, and so:

S	T	U	R		
60	400	6	200	=	666.

Though not explaining the basis for these numerical equivalents "in Chaldee," Hislop goes on to say that Saturn or Nimrod was "identical" with Janus; that the name Janus could be written as Eanus; that E-anush signified "the Man."[3] This, he supposes, fits the requirements of the prophecy—666 being the number of a *man* (Rev. 13:18). But when we consider that multiplied millions of creatures who have inhabited this planet fit the description "man," this hardly seems like a major point of identification!

This kind of "proof" carries about as much weight as finding 666 in the presidential names Ronald (6) Wilson (6) Reagan (6)— or George (6) Walker (6) Bush Jr (6)!

Though 666 is by far the best-known number for the Beast, there is no doubt whatsoever—as numerous Biblical scholars have pointed out—that "some very respectable manuscripts have *616* for the number."[4] While it is not our purpose here to argue for the validity of 616, this does bring us to another interesting twist. If we take the name "The Rev. Alexander Hislop," exactly as it appears on the title page of his book, the letters that have numerical value as Roman numerals count up to exactly 616!

THE REV	A	L	E	X	A	N	D	E	R	H	I	S	L	O	P	
		5		50	10		500			1		50			= 616

This does not, of course, make Hislop the Beast of Revelation! We only mention this to demonstrate that obtaining 666 (or 616) from a name, does not provide any conclusive identification. It is only one piece of the prophetic puzzle, not the complete picture.

1. *The Pulpit Commentary,* vol. 22, p. 337.   2. Hislop, p. 269.   3. Ibid., pp. 271, 272.   4. *Clarke's Commentary,* vol. 6, p. 964, Preface to The Revelation.

Chapter Five

BABYLONIAN SYMBOLISM?

The cross, as a symbol of Christ's death, is widely used by Christians of nearly all denominations. But Hislop claims the cross really came from Babylon and is the symbol of Tammuz!

> The same sign of the cross that Rome now worships was used in the Babylonian Mysteries....That which is now called the Christian cross was originally no Christian emblem at all, but was the mystic Tau of the Chaldeans and Egyptians—the true original form of the letter T—the initial of the name of Tammuz i.e. **†**.[1]

In times past, supposing that Hislop's complicated arguments were sound, I passed on this statement about the cross. I was not alone in this, even W. E. Vine in his *Expository Dictionary of New Testament Words* echoed it, saying the two beamed cross "had its origin in ancient Chaldea, and was used as the symbol of the god Tammuz...the initial of his name," so that the "T, in its most frequent form, with the cross-piece lowered, was adopted to stand for the cross of Christ."[2]

Because of Hislop's teachings, some have supposed the Babylonians worshipped a cross, wore crosses suspended from their necks, and displayed crosses on their temples—all in honor of Tammuz. This is simply not true.

Hislop gives no evidence the cross was a distinctive religious object in Babylon, but cites examples in *other* countries. These examples are varied in style and unrelated in purpose—with nothing to suggest a common origin. He mentions some large stone

---

1. Hislop, p. 197.   2. Vine, *An Expository Dictionary of New Testament Words*, p. 256.

crosses in Mexico, dedicated to the "god of rain," that were there prior to the arrival of Roman Catholic missionaries.[1] But, as *Hastings' Encyclopedia of Religion and Ethics* explains: "It is now known that these crosses were designed in allusion to the four quarters from which rain comes, and consequently to the winds that blow from the four cardinal points."[2] As such, they had nothing to do with the initial letter of Tammuz, no connection with Babylon, or with the cross as it is understood by Christians today!

Supposing that Bacchus was the same as Tammuz, Hislop reproduces the accompanying drawing of Bacchus (from Smith's *Classical Dictionary*), pointing out "crosses" on the head-band of "the Babylonian Messiah."[3] This obviously rests on no better evidence than an artist's conception!

In other examples, as in the accompanying illustration, Hislop says the cross was found upon garments prior to the Christian era.[4] That the cross design was used in the ancient world is no surprise—so were crescents, circles, squares, curves, straight lines, wavy lines, angles, triangles, and combinations thereof! The book *Decorative Patterns of the Ancient World* confirms this point with 3,064 drawings. There is no reason to suppose the cross design was more prominent than others.

If, at some time or place, someone actually worshipped a cross as a symbol of Tammuz, still, it was not Tammuz that died on a cross for our sins. No one has ever received Tammuz as his

1. Hislop, p. 199. 2. *Hastings' Encyclopedia of Religion and Ethics,* article: "Cross," p. 325 3. Hislop, p. 199. 4. Ibid., p. 198, from Wilkinson's *Ancient Egyptians.*

personal Savior and experienced a changed life. But "if any man be in *Christ,* he is a new creature: old things are passed away; behold, all things are become new"! (2 Cor. 5:17).

In my earlier Christian experience, when I came to realize the cross design was used in pre-Christian times and that the cross itself (as an instrument of death) was regarded as "the accursed tree," a device of torture and "shame" (Heb. 12:2), I supposed the cross could not truly be a Christian symbol. But this fails to take into account that *bad* can become *beautiful* through Jesus Christ! As *Hastings' Encyclopedia of Religion and Ethics* has phrased it: "The fact that Jesus suffered death on the cross has converted this infamous figure into a symbol of resurrection and salvation."[1]

Even the *place* where the cross was located, "Calvary" (Lk. 23:33), meaning place of a *skull,* has taken on an entirely new significance, so that we sing:

Mercy there was great and grace was free,
Pardon there was multiplied for me,
There my burdened soul found liberty,
At *Calvary!*

If we allow that Calvary (skull) can acquire a new signifi-cance, certainly the *cross* of Calvary, can do the same. The cross itself was not glorious and no one supposed it was. But because of Christ, it becomes glorious, so that even Paul says he *gloried in the cross* (Gal.6:14).

A church where I spoke some years ago, when singing "The Old Rugged Cross," would change the words. Instead of singing, "I will cling to the old rugged cross," they said, "I will cling to the *Christ* of the cross." Though well-intended, this change in wording is not really necessary. In the normal use of language, a single word can include a larger meaning, as when Paul spoke of the "cup" of the Lord or the Lord's "table" (1 Cor. 10:21). This was also the case when he said he gloried in the "cross" (Gal. 6:14). It included that for which the cross stood: Christ's death on the cross, shedding his blood for our sins. In other places he spoke of men being reconciled to God "by the cross" (Eph. 2:16), and of making

1. *Hastings' Encyclopedia of Religion and Ethics,* article: "Cross."

57

"peace through the blood of his cross" (Col. 1:20). It was not necessary to always say "the Christ of the cross," for this linkage was already established.

Believing that the commonly recognized shape of the cross came from the initial letter of Tammuz, some suppose Jesus did not die on a "cross" at all—that it was a post, a simple torture stake. While it is true that the Greek word translated "cross," *stauros,* means stake or post, it does not rule out that a cross piece was attached to it. Even today, if we use the word post—a wire fence may be fastened to it, a mail box mounted on it, or a sign attached to it—it is still a post. The word itself does not explain what is, or is not, attached to it.

I am not aware of even one Christian writer of the early centuries who supposed the cross was a simple torture stake. Instead, they spoke of the cross as having *"four* limbs pointing *above, below,* and *to both sides,* typifying 'the height, depth, length, and breadth' of the love of Christ, extending salvation to all (Eph. 3:18)."[2] Irenaeus mentioned extremities of the cross, "two in length, two in breadth."[3] Justin Martyr spoke of the cross as having "one beam placed upright" and "the other beam fitted on to it."[4] There is no reason to suppose that Justin—who became a martyr for Christ—fabricated this description in order to mix Tammuz worship with Christianity!

That the *stauros* had a cross piece is implied by the words of Thomas: "Except I shall see in his hands the print of the *nails,* and put my finger into the print of the *nails...*I will not believe" (John 20:25). Had Jesus died on a simple torture stake, his hands would have probably been driven through with one nail.

The crosses used by the Romans in the first century were of two types—one had the cross piece placed on top T, and the other had the cross piece lowered †.[1] That the cross of Jesus was the latter type is implied by the fact the "title" was attached *above* his head (Lk. 23:38).

1. *Harper's Bible Dictionary,* article: "Cross." 2. *Fausset's Bible Encyclopedia and Dictionary,* article: "Cross." 3. Irenaeus, *Against Heresies,* 2:24. 4. Justin, *Dialogue with Typho,* 91.

The teaching that it was not a cross on which Jesus died—that the cross is a symbol of Tammuz—only breeds confusion and questions: Do Christians who have a cross on their place of worship have some hidden agenda—are they really Tammuz worshippers in disguise? Or are they so ignorant they just don't know any better?

Frequently I drive a certain freeway from which can be seen, off in the distance, a little building with a cross on it. I would have assumed it was simply a house or structure used for some other purpose, except for the cross identifying it as a place of Christian worship. Multiplied thousands of Christians have built houses of worship over the years to which a cross has been attached. Not one ever put it up as a symbol of Tammuz! Not one, not ever. A cross on a church roof is not an antenna to attract Satanic power!

Go with me to another part of the world where the Moslem religion is prominent and the cross is seldom seen. We notice a place of religious activity, but instead of it being a church, it is a mosque. Instead of a cross, it is identified by a crescent moon. Then an amazing thing happens. One member turns to Jesus Christ and is gloriously converted. Soon others follow, until virtually the whole group experiences a great outpouring of the Holy Spirit. Now, as born again Christians, they continue to meet in the same building. One day, with great rejoicing, the crescent moon is taken down and up goes a cross on the roof! Could anyone be so warped as to say they were putting up a symbol of Tammuz?

There is strong evidence, and that *right within the Bible,* that the cross was *not* a recognized symbol of Tammuz! In Ezekiel 9, we read about a mark—apparently a cross—that was placed on the foreheads of the righteous: "...set a mark [*tau*] upon the foreheads of the men that sigh and that cry for all the abominations that be done" (Ezek. 9:4, 6). "According to the best interpretation of the text," says *The Pulpit Commentary,* "the mark seems to have been a *cross.*" The letter *tau* in Near Eastern languages could be written as + or †, and so it was not unnatural for early Christian writers, such as Origen and Tertullian, to see in this a type of the cross of Christ.[1]

---

1. *The Pulpit Commentary,* vol. 12, pp. 162,165 (Origen, in loc.; Tertullian, 'Adv. Marcion,' 111.22); *Harper's Bible Dictionary,* article: "Writing."

Now here is the point, and it is weighty: It was the *Lord* who ordered the ✝ to be placed on the foreheads of the righteous. If this was a recognized, evil, Babylonian symbol of Tammuz, why would the *Lord* designate this as the mark? Why would it be placed on the *righteous?* This was not a case of some wicked person placing a mark on the foreheads of wicked people. This  was the mark of God! If pagans worshipped the cross as the symbol of Tammuz, as Hislop speculates, placing *this* mark on the righteous would be especially inconsistent when considered *in context,* for it is only *eight verses* before that Tammuz worship is condemned! (Ezek. 8:14).

In my bedroom as a child, I had a cross on the wall that glowed in the dark. It was not a pagan symbol for me. It symbolized the cross of Jesus Christ. There are millions of people around the world who recognize the cross as a symbol of the cross of Jesus Christ. What possible purpose could be served by promoting the idea it represents the pagan god Tammuz?

Over the years I have had the opportunity to speak in hundreds of churches, many of which had a cross on the roof, above the platform, or on the pulpit. After I spoke one night, a man I had invited to attend, said I was preaching behind "the mark of the beast." I had not noticed, but there was a cross on the front of the pulpit! The meetings continued for several nights and were a blessing to all who attended. But not for this man. He never came back.

I know of a young man in prison who has received Christ, but refuses to attend the chapel services with fellow Christians. The reason? The chapel has a *cross* on the wall. He said he will not assemble where they display the emblem of *Satan!*

Does it seem incredible that anyone would think the cross is the emblem of Satan? This is exactly what Hislop taught! "At first it was the emblem of Tammuz, *at last it became the emblem of...Satan himself.*"[1] Just think, if this were true, then literally thousands and thousands of Christians meet beneath the sign of Satan!

1. Hislop, p. 281.

Now, admittedly, there have been abuses. Images of the cross have been used in superstitious and idolatrous ways by some, especially in centuries past. Even some Roman Catholic writers have deplored this, one going so far as to say that the cross "has received a worship similar, if not equal, to that of Christ; this sacred wood is adored almost equally with God Himself."[1] Such idolatrous use of the cross, or any other object, is wrong. But going to the other extreme—holding a dogmatic anti-cross position—can also be unfruitful and wrong!

A group of Christian young people attended a retreat in the mountains. At a lovely spot, beneath pine trees overlooking the

valley below, they met for daily devotions and prayer. Two of the young men decided to form a cross from tree limbs and placed it there. Someone else, taking pieces from a bush, twisted them into a "crown of thorns" and hung it on the cross. To them, this simple design provided a symbol of Christ's sufferings and death. There are some, however, who would consider this cross as "pagan," and, to them, the addition of the *round* crown of thorns would make it even worse! They suppose round images are symbols of the sun-god Baal!

It is true, of course, there were ancient people, including backslidden Israelites, who worshipped "sun-images" (2 Chron. 34:4, margin), as illustrated in the old woodcut given here. For obvious reasons, many idolatrous sun-images were *round* in shape—but this cannot mean everything round is a pagan sun-image! Years

ago I knew a fine Christian man who was no doubt very sincere and loved the Lord. But having read Hislop's book, he came to believe our whole society is permeated and defiled by pagan sun

---

1. *Hastings' Encyclopedia of Religion and Ethics*, article: "Cross," p. 328.

symbols. It became an obsession with him. Everywhere he looked he saw them. He compiled a scrapbook with all kinds of examples—clippings that ranged from "happy faces" to the insignia of the Southern Pacific Railroad!

I have read articles that condemn ball-shaped Christmas tree ornaments which are often red in color. Because they are "round," they supposedly symbolize the sun or Baal, while "red" is the color of sin (Isa. 1:18). But by this reasoning, we should not eat apples —they also are red and round! God made many things round: apples and oranges, grapefruit and grapes, the sun and the moon—and the earth itself! If "round" is wrong, it could be argued that a child should not be allowed to play with a ball; and besides, the same letters that spell "ball" spell "Baal"!

Some suppose rings, including wedding rings, are pagan because they are *round.* It does not seem to occur to them that a ring *has* to be round to fit on a round finger! If in some cultures rings had a pagan or magical significance, this has no bearing on rings in general. A wedding ring is a recognized symbol of marital unity and faithfulness—a good symbol. Jesus himself gave the story of the Prodigal Son who, upon returning to Father's House, was given a ring (Lk. 15:22). If a ring is evil, the point of this parable would be seriously confused.

If a ring is evil because it is *round,* what about a crown? The *Biblical* writers repeatedly use a crown as a symbol of good! Believers are "a crown of glory in the hand of the Lord, and a royal diadem" (Isa. 62:3); Christ is pictured with "many crowns" (Rev. 19:12); and the Christian's reward is a "crown of glory that fades not away" (1 Peter 5:4). Crowns are round so they will fit on the

head. Nevertheless, Hislop still gives somewhat of a negative twist to crowns, saying that Kronos or Saturn, whom he identifies with Nimrod, was "the first before all others that wore a crown."[1]

1. Hislop, p. 53.

Hislop says that Roman Catholic priests and monks "at their consecration, receive the circular tonsure, thereby identifying them, beyond all possibility of doubt, with Bacchus" or Nimrod.[1] But this point need not be pursued here, for the "tonsure was abolished by the Roman Catholic church in 1972."[2]

ROUND WAFER

Hislop also taught—and many of us echoed his words—that the *round* wafer some churches use in their communion services had a pagan origin:

> The *'round'* wafer, whose *'roundness'* is so important an element in the Romish Mystery, what can be the meaning of it, but just to show to those who have eyes to see, that the 'Wafer' itself is only another symbol of Baal, or the Sun.[3]

What is he saying—that centuries ago some Roman Catholic priests gathered in a secret session and agreed to make communion wafers in a "round" shape in honor of the sun-god Baal?

"The importance which Rome attaches to the *roundness* of the wafer, must have a reason," Hislop says, "and that reason will be found, if we look at the altars of Egypt. 'The thin, *round* cake,' says Wilkinson, 'occurs on all altars'."[4] Wilkinson did make this statement,[5] *but* as he enlarges on this point, he goes on to say: "The cakes were of *various* kinds. Many were round, oval, or triangular; and others had the edges folded over....They also assumed the shape of leaves, or the form of an animal, a crocodile's head, or some capricious figure; and it was frequently customary to sprinkle them (particularly the round and oval cakes) with seeds."[6] *But Hislop did not bother to give us this information!*

The fact that Egyptians baked thin round cakes is no surprise. So did the Israelites: "Thin round cakes were baked on heated sand or flat stones."[7] These were called "loaves" in the Old Testament (Exod. 29:23, Judg. 8:5, etc.), translated from a Hebrew word meaning circle or *round,* the same word used to describe a large *round* coin![8]

1. Hislop, p. 222.   2. *Grolier Encyclopedia of Knowledge,* article: "Tonsure."   3. Hislop, p. 163.   4. Ibid., p. 160.   5. Wilkinson, *Ancient Egyptians,* vol. 5, p. 353.   6. Ibid., p. 365.   7. *Unger's Bible Dictionary,* article: "Bread."   8. *Strong's Concordance,* 3603.

Another word, translated "cakes" (Gen. 18:6. Exod 12:39, etc.), is also based on a word meaning "round."[1] The fact that "loaves," "cakes," or "wafers" were round, did not make them wrong. Wafers were prepared by the Levites and used in the consecration of Aaron and his sons to the priesthood (Ex. 29:2, 23; Lev. 8:26), in the sacrifice of the peace offering (Lev. 2:4; 7:12), and in the offering of the Nazarites (Num. 6:15,19). Had such examples been in a Babylonian book—instead of the Bible—Hislop might have cited *these* as examples of paganism!

While condemning "round" communion wafers as images of the sun-god Baal, Hislop fails to mention that the very manna given by the Lord was *round!* "Upon the face of the wilderness there lay a small ROUND thing...And Moses said unto them, This is the bread which the Lord hath given you to eat" (Exod. 16:14). Did the *Lord* give his people a symbol of the sun-god Baal?

At the Last Supper, Jesus "took bread...brake it, and said, Take, eat..." (1 Cor. 11:23, 24). But this does not constitute any "command" about the *shape* of bread to be used, one way or the other. If we build doctrines on incidental details, one might argue that *women* should not take communion since only *men* were at the Last Supper! Only *apostles* were present—really a "closed communion"—so should only apostles partake? They all drank from the same cup, so is it wrong to use individual cups? They had all eaten a meal together, so must a meal be served before communion is received? By the

custom of the time, they were in a *reclining* position around the table (John 13:25), so would this mean communion should not be served to people who *sit* in a church pew? When Jesus washed the disciples' feet (John 13:5), is it not probable the basin into which he poured water was *round?* Would baptism in a *round* pool be invalid? What if a church meets in a *round* building? What if the communion were

1. *Strong's Concordance,* 5692, from 5746.

64

served from a *round* table? Let's face it: the shape is not the important thing! Within the framework of Christian "liberty," the attitude of the heart is more important than details that divide and distract (1 Cor. 8:9, Gal. 5:1, Rom. 14:14-17).

There can be no doubt that Hislop spent considerable time in his efforts to find pagan origins, which makes the following statement quite significant: "There is no evidence, so far as I have been able to find, that, in the Babylonian system, the thin round cake...was ever regarded in any other light than as a *symbol*," nor did they believe it was "changed into the god whom it represented."[1] If so, Roman Catholics did not get the doctrine of transubstantiation from Babylon! On the other hand, it is the Protestants who regard the communion bread as a symbol! Did *they* get this from Babylon? In reality, Babylon had nothing to do with it either way!

The Jerusalem Temple included a molten sea "ten cubits from brim to brim, *round* in compass...under it was the similitude of oxen" (2 Chron. 4:2, 3). Had this been featured in a temple at Babylon, instead, Hislop would have undoubtedly condemned this "round" molten sea as being pagan. And the oxen beneath it, what could they be but symbols of Osiris, the Egyptian Nimrod![2]

Oxen and garlands are mentioned in connection with the pagan worship of Jupiter (Acts 14:13). A "garland" or "wreath" is *round*. Augustine tells about a pagan ceremony in which a wreath was placed on a phallic replica: "During the festival of Liber, this obscene member...was carried with great honor...and brought to rest in its own place; on which unseemly member it was necessary that the most honorable matron should place a *wreath* in the presence of all the people."[3] Based on such things, some have supposed *every* use of a wreath is wrong. They especially target a

---

1. Hislop, p. 259.   2. cf. Ibid., p. 45.   3. Augustine, *The City of God*, Book 7:21.

"Christmas wreath" as being evil! But an idola-
trous use of a wreath and a wreath used as a
decoration, are two different things! The proof is
simple—and Biblical! The two pillars in front of
the Temple of God each had a "wreath" (2 Chron.
4:12, 13), and were also decorated with round
pomegranates (1 Kings 7:20)! These things were
not displeasing to God, for when the Temple was dedicated, *He*
chose to fill it with such glory that the priests could not stand to
minister! (2 Chron. 5:14). *He* did not consider the round wreaths,
round pomegranates, and round molten sea as symbols of Baal!

In a letter to me, Scott Klemm, a high school teacher, challeng-
ing the accuracy of some of Hislop's assertations, made up the
following statements to make a point—what Hislop might have said
about one of our pennies:

> Look closely at a brand
> new penny. One can't
> help but notice it has
> the *shape* and *color* of
> the *sun.* See the words
> "one cent." The term
> cent is derived from
> "centurion," a Roman army commander. It is a known historic
> fact that Mithraism was most popular among the Roman army
> and the merchant class.
>
> Now observe the picture of the Lincoln Memorial. Did you
> know that it's a replica of the Roman Temple of Saturn, and
> that Saturn is the Roman name for the Babylonian Tammuz,
> the sun-god? Is it a coincidence that this pagan temple first
> began to appear on the penny when John F. Kennedy (the first
> Roman Catholic president) came to office?
>
> Most people don't realize that the penny is a symbol of the round,
> sun-shaped wafer used in the Roman Catholic mass, and herein
> lies the answer to the mystery of the "Mark of the Beast."
> Throughout the world similar Romanist symbols of the sun are
> used as legal tender. Revelation 13:17 says, "No one can buy or
> sell unless he has the mark." In Germany, a coin is actually called
> a mark!

CIRCLE OF LIGHT

The circle, Hislop says, was "the emblem of Tammuz," a pagan sun symbol, "and the circle of light around the head of the so-called pictures of Christ was...borrowed from the very same source."[1] As an example of this pagan usage, he gives the accompanying drawing of Circe, "the daughter of the sun." Because Roman Catholics portray Mary the same way, he takes this as proof they do not really worship Mary, but "that very Babylonian queen who set up Nimrod"![2]

While it is true that the round glow of light, sometimes called a glory, halo, or nimbus, was used in Hellenic and Roman art to encircle the heads of gods, heroes, and other distinguished persons, the symbol itself is not evil. Light, quite naturally, forms a *circular glow*. If an artist is seeking to portray a saintly person from whom the light of God shines, the round glow of light is not unrealistic nor unbiblical.

In the Bible, when an angel appeared to the shepherds, "the *glory* of the Lord shown *round* about them" (Lk. 2:9). The Greek word here is *perilampo,* meaning "halo." It is based on *peri* (cf. peripheral) meaning "around," and *lampo* (cf. lamp), "to radiate brilliancy."[3]

As the wise men followed the star to Bethlehem, it "went before them, till it came and stood over where the young child was" (Matt. 2:9), or an alternate reading, cited by Adam Clarke, says it stood "over the *head* of the child." He goes on to say that "probably this gave the first idea to the ancient painters, of representing Christ in the manger, with a glory surrounding his head."[4]

1. Hislop, p.222.   2. Ibid., pp. 87, 88.   3. *Strong's Concordance,* 4034, 4012, 2989.
4. *Clarke's Commentary,* vol. 5, p. 46.

When Jesus was transfigured before his disciples on the mountain, "they saw his glory...his face did shine as the sun" (Lk. 9:32; Matt. 17:2). In Heaven, his countenance is "as the sun shining" (Rev. 1:16). Paul spoke of glorious light shining "in the face of Jesus Christ" (2 Cor. 4:6), while other verses mention the light of his countenance (Ps. 4:6, 89:15).

At the empty tomb, the face of an angel radiated a glorious brightness (Matt. 28:3). In Revelation a mighty angel with a face "as it were the sun" is described (Rev. 10:1). Jesus said the righteous will "shine forth as the sun" in the kingdom of God, while Daniel said they "shall shine as the brightness of the firmament" (Matt. 13:43; Dan. 12:3). And, of course, there is the notable example of the bright, glorious light that shown "from the face of Moses" (2 Cor. 3:7).

If any of these Biblical examples were to be illustrated in a drawing, a round glow of light would be appropriate. In another form, artists have sometimes used a crown-like circle of light just above the head of a saintly person. This too is in harmony with the scriptures which mention "a crown of glory" the brightness of which "fades not away" (1 Pet. 5:4; Isa. 62:3).

The sun has commonly been portrayed with "rays" of light extending from it, in somewhat the same way that spokes of a wheel extend outward forming a circle. The word "ray," consequently, provides the basis of "radius," the word used to designate the distance from the center to the edge of a circle.[1] In the accompanying present-day illustration, the encircling rays show which signal light is "on," compared to those that are "off." It is a simple, natural, normal, recognized method of illustration. It is not "pagan." For the purpose of illustration, then, to place rays of light extending forth from a dove representing the Holy Spirit, a communion cup, the cross, a Bible, or the woman "clothed with the sun" (Rev. 12:1), is not paganism, even though pagans used the same artistic style.

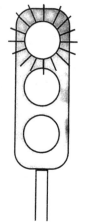

1. Skeat, *A Concise Etymological Dictionary of the English Language*, etc.

Artists have depicted Jesus in literally thousands of drawings, some of which have included the round glow of light. Portions from two old drawings are included here to illustrate the crown-type

circle of light and rays of light around the head of Jesus. I realize that such pictures look "pagan" to some. But they are not, when rightly understood.

Over the years in the ministry, I have been reluctant to use pictures of Jesus, primarily because we don't know exactly what he looked like. However, I have come to see there is no need to carry this to an extreme. The fact that he was a man, a real person, tells us quite a bit. He had two eyes, two ears, two arms, two legs, and two feet. He had hair, nose, mouth, and teeth. The fact that Judas had to point him out (Matt. 26:48), indicates he was probably not overly tall like Saul (1 Sam. 9:2), or notably short like Zacchaeus (Lk. 19:3). His hair style, beard, and clothing were not radically different than the others he was with. Much of this can be beneficially conveyed in drawings, even though we do not know exact features. There is no need to visualize him as "nothing."

There are people so adamant against "images," they suppose that something like a can of peaches—with a picture of peaches on the label—may be idolatrous. So they tear off the labels! I have known people who don't believe in having a camera because it makes an image. They have thrown away all their photographs, even those of family. I read once about a cult that did not believe in having mirrors—because mirrors make an image! Such strictness is not God's requirement (cf. Acts 15:28).

The drawing given here is an artist's concept of Peter's deliverance from prison by an angel (Acts 12:6-11). The bright light radiating from the angel is in harmony with scripture (cf. Rev. 10:1) and, on this occasion, a supernatural "light" that broke the darkness of the prison is specifically mentioned. It should be noticed, also, that the artist has pictured the angel with *wings.* In such drawings, this clearly distinguishes which is the angelic being. Nevertheless, this has been ridiculed by some who suppose the whole idea of wings came from paganism!

According to Hislop, a synonym for *gheber* (the Hebrew word translated "mighty" in the phrase "Nimrod was a *mighty* one"), "also signified a 'wing'." He supposes, therefore, that Nimrod "was

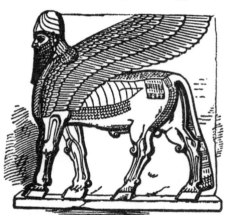

represented with great and wide-expanding wings" and that the accompanying drawing was intended to represent Nimrod.[1] But the word *gheber,* a common word, appearing in the Old Testament 157 times, is never translated "wing," nor could "wing" in any sensible way be substituted in these references.

Hislop even tries to link Nimrod with a fable about "wings" from far away Tahiti! The earth and the heavens were once bound together with cords, the fable says, but these were severed by a multitude of dragon-flies whose "wings" bore an important share

1. Hislop, p. 38.

70

in the great work. "Is there not here a reference to Nimrod's 'mighties' or 'winged ones'?" Hislop asks. He then tries to make the Babylonian connection—via Egypt—because the name of the Tahitian god of war, Oro, is similar to the name Horus![1]

Because the Bible represents angels as "flying" between heaven and earth (Rev. 8:13; Lk. 1:26; 2:15), it is not unrealistic to picture them as having *wings*. If some would object that angels do not need wings to fly, we would point out that neither do they need a ladder. Yet when God gave a dream to Jacob, he did not hesitate to use the symbol of a ladder: "...behold a ladder set up on the earth, and the top of it reached to heaven: and behold the angels of God ascending and descending on it" (Gen. 28:12).

Now it is true that angels often appeared as men (Acts 1:10) —with no indication of them having wings. Consequently, some people "entertained angels *unaware*" (Heb. 13:2), which could not have been the case if they all had wings. But in other Biblical references, there are angelic beings who are described as having wings. The holy place of the Temple featured cherubim with spread wings (2 Chron 5:7,8). Isaiah spoke of the seraphim, each having six wings (Isa. 6:2). Even *God*—symbolically of course—is represented as having wings: "...under his wings shalt thou trust"! (Ps. 91:4). Wings are not an evil symbol.

PAGAN CANDLES?

Based on examples that range from some Buddhists in Ceylon to an obscure tribe "near the Lake Baikai in Siberia," Hislop says that the use of lamps and wax-candles in the Roman Catholic Church came from paganism.[2] He fails to mention, however, that such were also used by *the people of God* in the Old Testament. By divine command, lamps were "to burn continually" in the sacred precincts of the Tabernacle (Lev. 24:2-4). Later, in Solomon's Temple, ten golden lamps burned in front of the oracle (1 Kings 7:49). From the early celebrations of Yom Kippur to present-day observances, Jews light candles on the eve of the Sabbath and other sacred days. Their commemoration of restored Temple worship following the defeat of Antiochus Epiphanes—called the Feast of

1. Hislop, p.54.   2. Ibid., pp. 191-193.

71

Dedication or Feast of Lights—was attended by Jesus in Jerusalem (John 10:22) and is observed today by the lighting of candles.

In the Scriptures, *light*—whether from a candle, lamp, or the sun—represents *good* (1 Thess. 5:5). "God is light" (John 1:5). Christians "walk in the light" (1 John 1:7), wear "an armor of light" (Rom. 13:12), are called "the children of light" (1 Thess. 5:5), "saints in light" (Col. 1:12), "his marvelous light" (1 Peter 2:9). The inner spiritual light of a believer is likened to "the bright shining of a candle" (Lk. 11:36). The Psalmist said the Lord will "light my candle" (Ps. 18:28). John the Baptist was "a burning and a shining light" (John 5:35). The seven churches of Revelation were symbolized by seven candlesticks, with Christ in the midst of them (Rev. 1:20; 2:1). Had candles or lamps been considered evil, this symbolism would have been entirely out of place!

But Hislop attempts to connect candles with *Nimrod!* He tells us that Nimrod, after his death, came to be worshipped as the Sun-

god, who "under the name of Mithra, was exhibited in sculpture as a Lion; that Lion had a Bee represented between his lips."[1] For this, he gives the accompanying illustration. Now if any ask what this has to do with candles, here it is, according to Hislop: the Babylonians believed Nimrod was the Sun-god, the Sun-god was Mithra, Mithra was represented as a lion, the lion had a bee in its mouth, bees make wax and *wax is used to make candles!*

Does this make wax evil? Other products from the bee such as *honey* and the *honeycomb* are highly regarded in the Scriptures (Prov. 24:13; Exod. 3:8; Psalms 19:10). If, as Hislop says, the *bee* was a symbol of the goddess Diana, and her chief priest was called the *king-bee*,[2] is this really some deep teaching proving the pagan origin of wax candles?

1. Hislop, p. 194.   2. Ibid., p.195.

Ah, but Hislop finds deeper meanings yet! "The bee between the lips of the Sun-god," he says, "was intended to point him out as 'the Word;' for *dabar*, the expression which signifies in Chaldee a 'bee,' signifies also a 'word'."[1] Now it is true the Hebrew *dabar* —used 1,445 times in the Old Testament—is often translated "word." Whether "in Chaldee" it ever meant *bee,* I don't know. But what if it did? Hislop reads a lot into this, saying "the idea intended to be conveyed" is that Nimrod or Mithra claimed to be "the Word," a counterfeit of Him who was truly the Word, Jesus Christ! (John 1:1).

Having set forth this idea, Hislop quotes an obscure "Popish work" that mentions Christ as "that celestial Bee" who brings sweetness to a corrupted world.[2] He then asks from what source this association between Christ, "the Word," and a "bee" could have come. His answer: Because it is in "the Babylonian tongue" that "bee" also means "word," the idea *"must have been drawn from a Babylonian prayer-book"!* [3]

Did pagans use candles in their rituals? Of course they did. Even *The Catholic Encyclopedia* says: "We need not shrink from admitting that candles...were commonly employed in pagan worship."[4] Instead of rejecting wax candles because pagans used them, one might better ask if their use serves any fruitful purpose. Is this usage spiritually meaningful? Or has it degenerated into a superstitious form that obscures the genuine light and glory of God? We feel answers to these questions would be more to the point than whether Nimrod was pictured as a lion with a bee in his mouth!

PAGAN OIL?

Not only wax, but the practice of using *oil* while giving the last rites has come under Hislop's attack. He says this practice—known in the Roman Catholic Church as Extreme Unction—came from "the Chaldean Mysteries."[5] He then cites some disjointed examples involving oil. "Among the many names of the Babylonian god was the name 'Beel-samen,' 'Lord of Heaven'," he says. But "in Sanchuniathon" it means "Lord of *Oil.* "[6] Legend has it that the

1. Hislop, p. 194.   2. Ibid., p. 196.   3. Ibid., p. 197.   4. *The Catholic Encyclopedia,* article: "Candles."   5. Hislop, p.165.   6. Ibid., p. 165.

body of Belus was preserved in his sepulchre, until the time of Xerxes, floating in *oil*.[1] People who consulted the oracle of Trophonius were rubbed over their whole body with *oil*.[2] In Rome the "statue of Saturn" was "made hollow, and filled with oil."[3] The olive branch was a symbol of "the Chaldean god,"[4] and olives produce *oil!*

Despite the disjointed nature of these examples of oil used in paganism, Hislop concludes: "From this source, *and this alone,* there can be no doubt came the 'extreme unction' of the Papacy."[5] But if using oil is pagan, this same argument could be used to criticize the *apostles* who "anointed with *oil* many that were sick, and healed them"! (Mk. 6:13).

The real issue here has nothing to do with Belus floating in oil or some oil-related name of a Babylonian god, but the proper interpretation of James 5:14, 15:

> Is any sick among you? let him call for the elders of the church; and let them pray over him, anointing him with oil in the name of the Lord: and the prayer of faith shall save the sick, and the Lord shall raise him up; and if he have committed sins, they shall be forgiven him.

Does this passage refer to last rites—anointing with oil and the prayer of faith to "save" the sick person, whereby his sins will be "forgiven," and he will be "raised up" *in the resurrection* at the last day—or does it refer to prayer whereby he is "raised up" from his sick bed *now?* Some, in a sense, have accepted both viewpoints: while holding the belief in prayer for healing, they also point out that calling for prayer is not inappropriate in one's dying moments, if this is possible, or at any other time in life.

It should be pointed out, however, for the true Christian, prayers offered at the hour of death are not for salvation. For him, that matter is already settled, so that with confidence he can say with Paul: "I *know* whom I have believed, and am *persuaded* that he is able to keep that which I have committed unto him against that day" (2 Tim. 1:12).

---

1. Hislop, p. 166.   2. Ibid.   3. Ibid.   4. Ibid.   5. Ibid., p. 167.

Chapter Six

PAGAN CONSPIRACY?

For centuries, Christians of varying denominations have used the letters I.H.S. as a monogram of Jesus Christ. These letters—an abbreviated form of the name Jesus in Greek—are sometimes used on communion wafers, vestments, or church furniture as a Christian symbol. But Hislop implies that the letters I.H.S. came from paganism!—another conspiracy to mislead Christians:

> To a Christian these letters are represented as signifying, *"Iesus Hominum Salvator,"* "Jesus the Savior of men." But let a Roman worshipper of Isis (for in the age of the emperors there were innumerable worshippers of Isis in Rome) cast his eyes upon them, and how will he read them? He will read them, of course, according to his own well-known system of idolatry: *"Isis, Horus, Seb,"* that is, "The Mother, the Child, and the Father of the gods,"—in other words, "The Egyptian Trinity."[1]

In this statement, Hislop assures us that the "innumerable" worshippers of Isis would *"of course"* take these letters to mean Isis, Horus, and Seb, but he provides no documentation—only three pagan names beginning with the letters I.H.S. As far as we can determine, these letters were never used as a *monogram* by pagans.

The time frame for Hislop's statement is "the age of the emperors...in Rome." But "the familiar monogram I.H.S was first popularized by St. Bernardine of Siena in the early fifteenth century."[2] This would have been *centuries* after the age of the emperors. So where is the connection?

1. Hislop, p. 164.   2. *The Catholic Encyclopedia*, article: "Monogram of Christ," vol. 10, p. 489.

Hislop refers to Isis, Horus, and Seb as *"The* Egyptian Trinity,"* as though there were only one Egyptian Trinity. Actually, Egypt had many different groupings of gods and goddesses—pairs, triads, and larger groups. Later, he states that "the *favorite* Triad" or Trinity in Egypt was that of "two mothers and the son"—Isis, Nepthys, and Anubis.[1] We find ourselves asking: Was Isis a member of two different "Trinities"?

On the subject of the Trinity, in another place Hislop says Roman Catholics are taught that *Mary* is a member of the Trinity —that the Melchites, at the Nicene Council, taught the Trinity consists of "the Father, *the Virgin Mary,* and the Messiah their son."[2] If there was a group that held this view at the Nicene Council, this was clearly not the position that was taken by the Council itself. I have never known even one Roman Catholic who believes the Trinity consists of the Father, Mother, and Son. All, so far as I am aware, believe the Trinity consists of the Father, Son, and Holy Spirit.

Instead of Isis, Horus, and Seb being "The Egyptian Trinity" —or any Trinity at all—I strongly suspect that Hislop placed these three names together, *and in this order,* simply so the letters I.H.S. would support his point.

The company that bottles Royal Crown Cola might use the letters R.C.C. Suppose someone said: "Oh, they want you to believe that the letters R.C.C. stand for 'Royal Crown Cola,' but actually they stand for 'Roman Catholic Church'"!

The initial letters for the American Baptist Convention are A.B.C. Suppose someone said these letters "really" stand for Aphrodite, Bacchus, and Cupid! Would this make it so?

The Seventh-Day Adventist church—whose intent would certainly not be to promote paganism—is commonly referred to by the letters S.D.A. By using Hislop's method, consider what could be done with these letters:

These letters are represented as signifying, "Seventh-Day Adventist." But let an ancient pagan worshipper of the Mother Goddess cast his eyes upon them, and how will he read them?

1. Hislop, p. 307.　2. Ibid., p. 89.

76

He will read them: "Semiramis, Diana, and Astarte"—a triad of pagan goddesses. Was not the Adventist church greatly influenced by a woman—Ellen G. White? Is not the family plot where she is buried at Battle Creek, Michigan, marked with an obelisk-shaped monument?[1] Is not the obelisk from pagan Egyptian idolatry, one of which stands before the central church of Roman Catholicism in *Rome?* Is it not true that the name Ellen G. White, if figured in *Roman* numerals, has a numerical value of 666?"[2]

My apologies here to many fine Seventh Day-Adventists—I only include this disjointed reasoning to illustrate the point.

I am not arguing for the use of the monogram I.H.S. More important than whether we use it—or do not use it—is that we don't bear false witness about something, simply because it may not be a common part of our belief system.

To use Greek letters as symbols of Jesus is not a pagan practice. Jesus himself is quoted as saying, "I am Alpha and Omega, the beginning and the end" (Rev. 1:8, 22:13). Alpha is the beginning letter of the Greek alphabet and Omega the end letter.[3]

"F I S H"

The early Christians used the Greek word *ichthus,* "fish," as an acrostic based on the initial letters of the words "Jesus Christ, Son of God, Savior."[4] This was not something they borrowed from paganism, but was probably a protest against the paganism of Roman Emperors, such as Domitian (A. D. 81-96) who took to himself a title meaning "Son of God." The Son of God to Christians was not Domitian, but Jesus Christ the Savior.

We know also that during the persecution era, the fish was a code symbol for Christians.[5] Upon coming in contact with another person, the outline of a fish might be drawn on the ground. If the other person were a Christian, he would then be able to identify a fellow believer in "Jesus Christ, Son of God, Savior."

1. White, *Ellen G. White, Messenger to the Remnant,* p. 127.   2. *The Babylon Connection?* p. 53.   3. The letters of the Greek alphabet are: **Alpha,** Beta, Gamma, Delta, Epsilon, Zeta, Eta, Theta, Iota, Kappa, Lambda, Mu, Nu, Xi, Omicron, Pi, Rho, Sigma, Tau, Upsilon, Phi, Chi, Psi, **Omega.**   4. *Harper's Bible Dictionary,* article: "Fish."   5. Ibid.

But Hislop, with no proof at all, says this widespread practice of using "fish" as a title of Christ was *"manifestly to identify him with Dagon"*![1] This is ridiculous. What purpose would it serve for Christians, or anyone else, to identify Christ with the fish-god Dagon? If the fish was a recognized symbol of Dagon at the time, how could it serve as a *code* symbol for persecuted Christians? The fact is, Dagon worship had died out long before—in the latter days of the Assyrian Empire—and was not contemporary with Christianity.[2]

Today, numerous dedicated Christians, as did early Christians, use the fish symbol. If it is seen on the back of an automobile, can anyone rightly say: "That person  is a worshipper of the fish-god Dagon"? Of course not. *If* the fish was ever used as a symbol for Dagon, it would have been so long ago, and by such a tiny segment of people, it could hardly have any bearing on what the symbol means now.

In ancient times, those who entered the temple of Dagon did not "tread on the threshold" (1 Sam. 5:5). Today, in keeping with a wedding custom, a groom may carry his new bride over the threshold into their new house. Does this make him a worshipper of Dagon? Of course not! Though there is a similarity—a threshold is involved—there is no connection.

PAPAL MITRE

Equally disconnected is the claim that the Pope wears the mitre of the fish-god Dagon. During the period that Hislop wrote, Austen Henry Layard, English traveler and archaeologist (1817-1894), became world-famous for his excavations in Assyria which he described in *Nineveh and Babylon*. Based on cylinders and monuments of that area, Layard's book included drawings of several different creatures, part man and part fish.

As Hislop read this book, one of these drawings grabbed his attention, as did the wording, "the head of the fish formed a mitre

1. Hislop, p. 247. 2. *Hastings' Encyclopedia of Religion and Ethics,* article: "Dagon."

above that of the man, whilst its scaly back and fanlike tail fell as a cloak behind, leaving the human limbs and feet exposed."[1] By comparing this drawing and description with the mitre worn by the Pope, the  similarity was apparent! This would cause Hislop to write:

> The Pope...wears the mitre of Dagon. The excavations of Nineveh have put this beyond all possibility of doubt....The two-horned mitre, which the Pope wears...is the very mitre worn by Dagon, the fish-god of the Philistines and Babylonians ....No one who examines his mitre, and compares it with the Pope's...can doubt for a moment that from that, and no other source, has the pontifical mitre been derived.[2]

But the excavations of Nineveh do not prove the mitre worn by the Pope is that of Dagon. Nineveh was destroyed around 612 B.C.— long *before* a pope wore any kind of mitre. And the ruins of Nineveh were not excavated until Layard did so in the mid-1800s A.D.—long *after* a pope started wearing a mitre. Where, then, is the connection?

Instead of the Roman Catholic mitre being fashioned from an image of Dagon, there is sufficient evidence to show its present shape *developed* over a period of centuries. *The Encyclopedia Britannica* points out it was originally a somewhat high conical

cap. About A.D. 1100 this gave place to a rounded one. Later a band of embroidery over the top tended to bulge up the soft material on either side, and these bulges became points or horns. From this the divided mitre emerged, and finally the mitre as it is presently known.[3]

1. Layard, *Nineveh and Babylon*, p. 343.   2. Hislop, p. 215.   3. *Encyclopedia Britannica*, article: "Mitre."

Today there are hats with a wide variety of styles and shapes—royal hats and religious hats, dunce hats and fishing hats, formal hats and casual hats, cowboy hats and space helmets! If one were to search long enough, he could probably find people of some ancient culture who wore a hat with a similar shape to any of these.

In the Old Testament, the high priest wore a mitre, which is generally understood to have been a turban (Lev. 16:4). But in the New Testament, writing to the Corinthians, Paul spoke of a man who prayed or prophesied as *not* having his head covered (1 Cor. 11:4). So without in any way arguing for the use of the ecclesiastical mitre, still, there is no reason to condemn it as the fish-head of Dagon!

BLACK GARMENTS

Like the mitre, the use of black clergy garments was a development. Originally, before the time of Constantine, "the priestly dress did not yet differ from the secular costume in form and ornament. The dress of daily life was worn at the offices of the Church."[1] Later, distinctive garments began to be worn by the clergy. By the 10th century, these garments in the Greek church were black, but it was not until the 15th century in France, and the 16th century in Italy, that black was in general use.[2]

Did the custom of wearing *black* clergy garments come from paganism? There were pagan priests, mentioned in the Bible as *Chemarims* (Zeph. 1:4)—a word that signifies to be made dark or black—who may have been so named because of the black garments they wore.[3] But it would be difficult to show any *connection* between these garments and those of the Roman Catholic priesthood. Centuries separate the two. It is not as though some popular, contemporary, pagan priesthood wore black in the 16th century, and compromising church leaders copied it.

If any suppose that wearing black comes from paganism, the same argument could be used against the cover on a Bible being black. Are we going to throw a Bible away because it has a *black* cover? Are we going to waste time preaching against black covered Bibles?

1. *The Catholic Encyclopedia,* article: "Vestments."   2. Tyack, *Historic Dress of the Clergy,* p. 22   3. *Clarke's Commentary,* vol. 4, p. 752.

Roman Catholics believe the two keys on the papal insignia symbolize the keys of spiritual authority that Christ gave to Peter: "I will give unto you the keys of the kingdom of heaven" (Matt. 16:19). But Hislop says that keys "were the symbols of two well-known Pagan divinities at Rome. Janus bore a key, and Cybele bore a key; and *these* are the two keys that the Pope emblazons on his arms as the ensigns of his spiritual authority"![1]

According to *The Encyclopedia Americana,* Janus, as god of doors, was sometimes represented with a key in his hand.[2] But this same encyclopedia, while giving numerous details about Cybele, says nothing about her having a key. At her birth, disappointed she was not a boy, king Maeon, her father, cast her aside on Mount Cybelus where she was nursed by lions and panthers. She invented fifes and drums, with which she cured the diseases of beasts and children. She is pictured as holding a staff in her right hand and a drum in her left—but nothing about holding a key is mentioned.[3]

Nevertheless, if a key was in some way associated with Cybele, and with Janus also, why insist it is these keys that decorate the papal insignia? If it is pagan to use "keys" as a symbol, it could be argued that the New Testament writers were pagans—and Jesus Christ also—for *He* is described as holding *keys!* (Rev. 1:18; 3:7).

EGYPTIAN PROCESSION

Hislop gives the accompanying drawing of an Egyptian monarch being carried in a procession.[4] Because the Pope has been

1. Hislop, p. 207.   2. *The Encyclopedia Americana,* article: "Janus."   3. Ibid., article: "Cybele."   4. Hislop, p. 214.

carried in the same way, he implies this custom was copied from paganism. But any evidence for this is weak. If we place a picture of Adolf Hitler riding in an open limousine next to a later picture of an American president riding in a similar vehicle, despite the similarity, there would be no reason to suppose the one was copied from the other. So is it here.

Without paved roads as we know them, a palanquin or "litter," as it is called in the Bible (Isa. 66:20), being *carried* by men, provided a smoother ride than a cart with wheels. Such was used in earlier times, not only for transporting kings and dignitaries, the rich and famous, but also the sick or elderly, and ladies. King Solomon had a palanquin decorated with silver, gold, and purple (Song of Sol. 3:9).[1] This ancient custom has for a long time been perpetuated in the Roman Church, by carrying the Pope in this manner. But I would assume the bullet-proof "Popemobile" is the most popular way now.

We have read accounts of the Pope being carried along, with great pomp and ceremony, as crowds of people bow to him, a practice in our estimation that does not reflect the humility of Jesus. Peter, it should be remembered, did not want people bowing to him (Acts 10:25,26; cf. Mk. 10:43). This, it seems to me, is a greater issue than what type of transportation is used.

FAN OF BACCHUS?

Hislop, describing a papal procession, says the Pope "was borne along on the shoulders of men, amid the gaping crowds, his head was shaded or canopied by two immense *fans*, made of peacocks' feathers."[2] He then refers us to the drawing of the Egyptian monarch being carried, who is also accompanied by a fan. This fan, he says, is the "Mystic fan of Bacchus"![3]

Immediately this suggests some sinister purpose. Bacchus, after all, was the god of wine and revelry; his festivals were marked by drunken orgies; his followers danced wildly and tore animals, and sometimes people, to pieces. For the Pope, then, to be accompanied by the "Mystic fan of Bacchus," certainly sounds evil. But

1. Though translated "chariot" (KJV), this is not the word so translated elsewhere; it literally means a moving couch.   2. Hislop, pp. 213, 214.   3. Ibid.

where is the proof? I have carefully checked the articles on "Bacchus" in numerous reference works. Not one, that I have seen, mentions anything about a "mystic fan of Bacchus."

One reason why an Egyptian sovereign was accompanied by a fan was to cool the air in that hot climate. There is nothing wrong with this! Would a preacher who has air conditioning in his car be less-spiritual than one who does not? Processional fans were also used to *drive away insects.* It has been said that the heathen used fans ritually—to fan the flames of their sacred fires. This may be true, but in the case before us, the fan was not for fanning flames, but flies! Why give a fan some evil meaning? Even Jesus, figuratively, is described as having a fan in his hand! (Matt. 3:12).

The drawing of the Egyptian monarch being carried in procession was reproduced by Hislop from Wilkinson's *Ancient Egyptians,* Plate 76. But Wilkinson gives another drawing that should be considered, Plate 86, which is titled: "A Procession in which Palm Branches are Strewed in the Way." One cannot help but recall the Triumphal Entry of Jesus, described in nearly the same wording, when people "took *branches of palm trees...*and *strewed them in the way"* (John 12:13; Matt. 21:8). Were they copying Egyptian paganism? Did they have "Scripture" for this custom? Regardless, Jesus did not rebuke them for honoring him in this manner; nor did the inspired gospel writers hesitate to record it! This should be carefully noted.

In the drawing of the Egyptian monarch, he is holding a *scepter,* similar to the one shown here.[1] But this is not necessarily an evil symbol; even Jesus Christ is described as holding a "scepter of righteousness" (Heb. 1:8). The crosier or shepherd's staff that is sometimes carried by the Pope or other Roman Catholic leaders is similar in shape.

Because Christ is "the great shepherd of the sheep" (Heb. 13:20), and his ministers are also called pastors or shepherds (Eph. 4:11; 1 Peter 5:2-4), a shepherd's staff is not an inappropriate

1. *Harper's Bible Dictionary,* article: "Scepter."

symbol. But according to Hislop, "this magic crook can be traced up directly to the first king of Babylon, that is Nimrod," citing an obscure reference to him as a "Shepherd-king."[1] Would this mean Nimrod carried a shepherd's staff? And what if he did? Even the *Lord* is represented as having a shepherd's staff (Psalms 23:4).

Attempting to give the crosier a Babylonian origin, Hislop says the accompanying illustration (from Kitto's *Biblical Cyclopedia*), "shows the crosier in its ruder guise."[2] But when we turn to the reference cited, Kitto says nothing about any crosier. He simply says this drawing, taken from a Babylonian cylinder, was included to illustrate the type of clothing worn, and makes no attempt to explain what the people were doing or holding![3]

Finally, citing a few obscure examples—from African negro deities made in the form of hooks, to idols in a Japanese temple with shepherds' crooks in their hands—Hislop concludes that "the crosier of the Pope, then...is neither more nor less than the magic rod of the priests of Nimrod"![4]

RELICS

Hislop also tries to link relics with Nimrod. "The worship of relics is just a part of those ceremonies instituted to commemorate the tragic death of Osiris or Nimrod, who...was divided into fourteen pieces," he says. When, later, the followers of Nimrod sought "for these dismembered *relics* of the great ringleader in idolatry, and to entomb them with every mark of devotion," it provided the basis for collecting bones and other objects which has continued for centuries in the Roman Catholic Church![5]

It will not be necessary here to go into details to show that many relics are not genuine—pieces of the cross, nails from the cross, the crown of thorns, bones of the donkey on which Jesus

1. Hislop, p. 217.   2. Ibid.   3. Kitto, *Biblical Cyclopedia*, vol. 1, p.272.   4. Hislop, p. 218.   5. Ibid. p. 179

rode, Joseph's carpenter tools, the cup from the Last Supper, Pilate's basin, specimens of hair from the Virgin Mary, etc. *The Catholic Encyclopedia* itself recognizes that *"many of the more ancient relics duly exhibited for veneration in the great sanctuaries of Christendom or even at Rome itself must now be pronounced to be either certainly spurious or open to grave suspicion."*[1]

But suppose the actual bones of Paul, or the robe of Jesus, or the ten commandments written on tables of stone were in our possession. Would it be proper to discard them as though they had no significance? Or would a better purpose be served if they were properly kept to the glory of God?

The basic idea of preserving significant things is not pagan. The Israelites preserved for future generations "the golden pot that had manna, and Aaron's rod that budded, and the tables of the covenant" (Heb. 9:4). The ark of the covenant that housed these things, was itself kept as a trophy of God's blessings (2 Sam. 6:17). Even twelve rocks from the Jordan river bed served as a memorial of Israel crossing over on dry ground (Josh. 4:2-7). The serpent of brass that Moses made was preserved for hundreds of years, but was later destroyed because it came to be used in an idolatrous way (2 Kings 18:4).

In view of these things, instead of a wholesale condemnation of all relics, we might better ask: Are they genuine? Do they serve some worthwhile purpose? Or are they used in superstitious ways?

The superstitious use of relics should be rejected. Relics known to be false should be rejected. *And,* saying the Roman Catholic Church has preserved relics *"because of Nimrod"* is also false, and should be rejected!

---

1. *The Catholic Encyclopedia*, article: "Relics."

Chapter Seven

FACT OR FABLE?

Though many of Hislop's claims about pagan origins cannot be confirmed by any reliable history book, he repeatedly gives the impression his arguments are based on recognized facts!

Hislop makes statements about Nimrod, Odin, Rhea, and others—all of which he says are "well-known."

"Nimrod...was the great war-god. Odin, as is **well-known,** was the same" (p. 312).

"Semiramis...it is **well-known,** was worshipped under the name of Rhea" (p. 21).

"It is **well-known** that Kronos...was Rhea's husband" (p. 31).

"Proserpine...**well-known** to be the wife of Pluto..." (p. 126).

"Janus...his **well-known** title 'Janus Tuens'..." (p. 27).

"The female divinity corresponding to Apis, is **well-known** as a spotted cow" (p. 45).

"It is **well-known** that the Brahmins...taught...they alone came from the mouth of the creative God" (p. 15).

"The Cyclops were **well-known** as cannibals" (p. 232).

"It is **well-known** that [Alexander the Great's mother said he was sprung] from Jupiter, in the form of a serpent" (p. 277).

Hislop cites various quotations that are not familiar to most of us, yet these are said to be "well-known."

"...the **well-known** line of Pope...'A mighty maze, but not without a plan'." (p. ix).

"Servius...after quoting the **well-known** expression, 'Mystica vannus Iacchi'..." (p. 139).

"...the **well-known** Moslem saying, 'Allar Akbar'..." (p. 317).

"'All human ills,' says Euripides, in a **well-known** passage, 'are washed away by the sea'." (p. 143).

"[Caesar's] **well-known** watchword, 'Venus Genetrix,' which meant that Venus was the mother of the Julian race" (p. 241).

"...the **well-known** expression *Ignis fatuus"* (p. 311).

Most of us have never even heard of names that Hislop mentions as being "well-known"!

"The **well-known** name Deucalion, as connected with the flood..." (p. 315).

"It is **well-known** Derketo and Atergatis are the same" (p. 86).

"...the **well-known**...name of Hephaistos" (p. 27).

"Nimrod...under the **well-known** name of Phaëthon..." (p. 230).

"It is **well-known** that Bimater, or Two-mothered, is one of the distinguishing epithets applied to Bacchus" (p. 307).

"Dionysus, as is **well-known,** is the Latin form of the Greek Dionusos" (p. 122).

Or consider these statements about things supposedly "well-known":

"It is **well-known** that the Minotaur...was half-man, half-bull" (p. 273).

"The Hebrew z, as is **well-known,** frequently, in the later Chaldee, becomes d" (p. 312).

"The sacred egg of Paganism...is **well-known** as the 'mundane egg'." (p. 109).

"These cuttings in the flesh...are **well-known** to have been practiced in the rites of Bellona" (p. 152).

"It is **well-known**" that Rome was saved "by the cackling of the geese...kept in the temple of Jupiter" (p. 101).

"...the **well-known** Greek word Até, which signifies 'error of sin'." (p. 273).

"Tur...Taurus...Turannus...**well-known** classical words" (p. 33).

"Thusht is the infinitive, and *ra* appended to it is...the **well-known** sign of the doer of an action" (p. 59).

"The **well-known** figure in the sphere called *Ariadnœa corona*, or 'Ariadne's crown'..." (p. 186).

Frequently Hislop throws out statements that "everyone" knows this or that:

"But of the existence of a goddess of fortifications, **everyone knows** that...goddess is Cybele" (p. 30).

"Now, **everyone knows** what was the name by which 'the Lord of the fly'...was called" (p. 279).

"**Everyone knows** that Homer's *odzos Areos*, or 'Branch of Mars,' is the same as the 'Son of Mars'." (p. 49).

"**Everybody** has heard of St. Swithin's day..." (p. 280).

It is not necessary here to challenge these statements, except to say that most are definitely *not* that "well-known" and *not* "everyone" knows them to be true. Since we don't want to be dummies, there is a tendency to accept such statements—*and arguments based on them*—without question. After all, they are "well-known"!

MANY REFERENCES

Another thing that seems to give a lot of credibility to Hislop's work is the use of many footnote references—"over 260 original sources of facts," a publisher's note says! But having put forth considerable effort to find many of the old books to which he refers, I have discovered that *the references often do not match his claims.*

Hislop says the appearance of the angel Gabriel to Mary is commemorated by Roman Catholics on "the 25th of March," but, "*that very day* now set down in the Popish calendar for the 'Annunciation of the Virgin' was observed in Pagan Rome in honor of Cybele, the Mother of the Babylonian Messiah."[1] But when we turn to the reference he cites, it is the *27th of March,* not the 25th, that is mentioned! Julian, on a military journey, arrived at

1. Hislop, p. 102.

88

Callinicum, and "there, *on the twenty-seventh of March,* the day on which at Rome the annual procession in honor of the Mother of the Gods takes place, and the carriage in which her image is carried is washed, as it is said, in the waters of the Almo, he celebrated the usual rites in the ancient fashion and spent the night in peaceful sleep."[1] We can assume the "Mother of the gods" referred to was Cybele, but she is not mentioned by name. There is nothing about her being "the mother of the *Babylonian* Messiah" and the date in March is *not* "that very day" Hislop says!

Hislop tells us that the historian "Tacitus gives evidence that the *Babylonian* goddess was worshipped in the heart of Germany."[2] But when we look up the reference, it mentions Isis, an Egyptian goddess. "In some parts of the country of the Suevians, the worship of Isis is established....The figure of a ship (the symbolic representation of the goddess) clearly shows that the religion was imported into the country."[3] A footnote says this was probably a German deity represented by a ship, which "led the Romans to mistake her for Isis." But whether it was a German deity or Isis an Egyptian deity, the text says nothing about "the *Babylonian* goddess"!

Hislop says the deified Semiramis was symbolized by a dove "with an olive branch in her mouth," and in her human form she was also portrayed *"bearing the olive branch in her hand."*[4] But  when we turn to the reference given, we have the accompanying illustration, and the words of Layard describing the ruins of Sinjar, the capital of an Arab principality: "On coins...this city is represented by a female wearing a mural crown surmounted by a centaur, seated on a hill."[5] Layard says nothing about the woman on this coin being Semiramis. Nothing is said about the branch she is holding being from an olive tree. The brief text does mention that Sinjar had palm trees.

Referring to Roman Catholics singing the *Miserēré,*[6] Hislop says: "Certain it is that much of the pathos of that *Miserēré*

1. Ammianus Marcellinus, Book 23:3.   2. Hislop, p. 81.   3. Tacitus, *Germania,* IX.   4. Hislop, p. 79.   5. Layard, *Nineveh and Babylon,* p. 250.   6. *Miserere,* a Latin term meaning *have mercy,* based on the Psalm 51 (Psalm 50 in the Douay Version).

depends on the part borne in singing it by the *sopranos;* and equally certain it is that Semiramis...enjoys the fame, such as it is, of having been the inventress of the practice from which *soprano singing* took its rise."[1]

But when we look up the reference, what Hislop calls "the practice from which soprano singing took its rise" is simply a statement by Ammianus Marcellinus, in passing, that "Queen Semiramis of old...was the first of all to castrate young males." It is commonly believed that eunuchs have a higher pitched voice, but to cite this as the origin for soprano singing does not seem justified. The reference itself does not mention soprano singing.[2]

"In the *Babylonian* system there was a symbolical death," Hislop says, "that all the initiated had to pass through."[3] But when we look up the reference, the initiation rite described is Egyptian, not Babylonian: "The candidate for initiation...was required to undergo the most severe ordeal, and to show the greatest moral resignation; but the ceremony of passing under the knife of the Hierophant, was merely emblematic of the regeneration of the *neophyte.* "[4] If the Egyptians got the idea from the Babylonians, this would make the point, but there is no indication of this in the reference.

Speaking of Nimrod, Hislop says: "He was worshipped in Babylon under the name of El-Bar....Under this name he has been found in the sculptures of Nineveh by Layard."[5] But when we turn to the reference given, this page is simply a list of "the Thirteen Great Gods of Assyria" as found on an upright tablet in cuneiform writing and translated as follows: Asshur, Anu, (?), San, Merodach, Yav, *Bar,* Nebo, Mylit, Dagon, Bel, Shamash, and Ishtar.[6] There is *nothing* to suggest the name "Bar" refers to Nimrod! In other places, Hislop has said some of these other gods on this list were Nimrod![7]

Hislop takes details about Phoroneus and applies them to Nimrod. He supposes that Nimrod, who gathered people into communities (Gen. 10:10), must be Phoroneus, whom legend says was the first to gather people into communities.[8] But when we actually

---

1. Hislop, p. 156.   2. Ammianus Marcellinus, Book 14:6.   3. Hislop, p. 236.   4. Wilkinson, *The Ancient Egyptians,* vol. 1, p. 267.   5. Hislop, p. 73.   6. Layard, *Nineveh and Babylon,* p. 629.   7. Hislop, pp. 24, 34, 44, 54, 246.   8. Ibid., p. 51.

read the reference Hislop gives, it does not fit Nimrod: "Another legend is that *the first man born in this country* [Greece] was Phoroneus, and that his father Inachus was not a man, but the *river of that name*....It was Phoroneus...who brought mankind together for the first time; for hitherto they had lived scattered and solitary. And the place where they first assembled was named the city of *Phoronicum.*"[1] But Nimrod was not the first man born in Greece. Nimrod's father was not a river. Nimrod's city was Babel, not Phoronicum!

To symbolize the "doctrine of the Trinity," Hislop says, the Babylonians "employed, as the discoveries of Layard prove, the equilateral *triangle,* just as it is well-known the Romish Church does at this day."[2] When we turn to the reference cited,[3] we find the drawing reproduced here, with a triangle in the upper left-hand  corner. It appears in a section of Layard's work describing various ancient engravings—this one from a Babylonian cylinder, cut in iron hematite. But Layard says *nothing about the triangular symbol!*

Hislop bases his argument against round communion wafers on Wilkinson's statement that "the thin, round cake occurs on all altars" in Egypt. But when we turn to Wilkinson's work, he says they *also* had cakes in the shape of an oval, triangle, leaves, crocodile's head, and other figures![4]

In another appeal to Wilkinson, Hislop says the 40 days of Lent came from paganism: "Such a Lent of forty days was observed in Egypt, as can be seen on consulting Wilkinson's *Egyptians.*"[5] But when we consult this reference, Wilkinson says Egyptian fasts "lasted *from seven to forty-two days,* and sometimes even a longer period: during which time they abstained entirely from animal food, from herbs and vegetables, and above all from the indulgence of the passions."[6] With as much credibility, we

1. Pausanias' *Description of Greece,* chap. 15.   2. Hislop, p. 16.   3. Layard, *Nineveh and Babylon,* p. 605.   4. See *The Babylon Connection?* p. 63.   5. Hislop, p. 105.   6. Wilkinson, *Ancient Egyptians,* vol. 1, p. 278

could say they fasted 7 days, 10 days, 12 days, or 42 days! Hislop's claim only appears to have validity because he used *partial* information.

If we base claims on partial information, we could even prove— from the Bible—*there is no God!* But when the entire statement is read, it has a different meaning: "The *fool* has said in his heart, There is no God" (Psa. 14:1).

WINTER SOLSTACE

"That Christmas was originally a Pagan festival, is beyond all doubt," Hislop says. "In Egypt, the son of Isis...was born *at this very time, 'about the time of the winter solstice'.*"[1] But when we check the reference he gives,[2] it does not back up his claim. It does say Isis gave birth to a son "about the time of the winter solstice," but this was a premature birth, causing him to be "lame in his lower limbs," and the Egyptians "celebrate the feast of his mother's delivery just after the Vernal Equinox"—*in Spring!* Taken in context, this obviously provides no origin for a *December* celebration.

In other places, Hislop would have us believe that Isis and her son Horus were but the Egyptian version of Semiramis and her son Tammuz, the Babylonian Messiah. But the son of Isis that was born "about the time of the winter solstice," as the reference clearly explains, was *Harpocrates—not* her older son Horus! But, avoiding any mention of this crucial point, Hislop offers a sweeping conclusion: "There can be no doubt, then, that the Pagan festival at the winter solstice—in other words, Christmas—was held in honor of the birth of the Babylonian Messiah"![3]

After making unsubstantiated statements like: "The Christmas tree, now so common among us, was *equally common* in Pagan Rome and Pagan Egypt,"[4] Hislop attempts to connect it with Nimrod! "The Christmas-tree is Nimrod *redivivus*—the slain god come to life again."[5] He says that Nimrod was the same as Melikerta,[6] and that "Melikerta, under the name of Palæmon" rode triumphantly on a fish, with the fir-tree in the background as his

1. Hislop, p. 93.   2. Wilkinson, *Ancient Egyptians*, vol. 4, p. 405.   3. Hislop, p. 102.
4. Ibid., p. 97.   5. Ibid., p. 98.   6. Ibid., p. 318.

ensign, which "came to be recognized in the character of the Christmas-tree."[1] For this he gives the accompanying illustration. But where is the connection? Repeatedly Hislop builds on some vague similarity, forming conclusions that are not verified by the source material he cites.

As though it had some bearing on the subject of the Christmas tree, Hislop says: "The mother of Adonis...was mystically said to have been changed into a tree, and when in that state to have brought forth her divine son."[2] In the fable to which he refers, a young girl, pregnant by her own father, prays to the gods; her feet begin to grow into the ground, becoming roots; she is turned into a tree, the bark of which splits open, and the baby is born.[3]

It is apparent that Hislop's examples are disjointed. First the Christmas tree was Nimrod, now it is a *woman!* "If the mother was a tree," Hislop continues, "the son must have been recognized as the 'Man the branch'."[4] This would prove little, in that "Branch" is used in the Bible as a righteous title (Zec. 3:8; 6:12). But Hislop supposes it means misletoe.

If a Christian family, playing in the snow, makes a large snowman—though it has the same features as an idol, I think most

would agree there is no idolatry involved. It is not an object of worship. There is no reason to suppose a Christmas tree is any different. If at some other time and place people actually worshipped trees, this is not the case of a Christian family that chooses to decorate with a Christmas tree today.

1. Hislop, p. 142.   2. Ibid., p. 97.   3. Ovid's *Metamorphasis*, 500-513.   4. Hislop, p. 97.   5. Ibid., p. 99.

Despite his "multitude of words" (Ecc. 5:3), Hislop fails to prove any Babylonian origin for Christmas. Instead, he veers off into some boring statements about boars—trying to show why the English eat a boar's head at Christmas. He says "the Phrygian Attis...was fabled to have perished...by the tusk of a boar."[1] But when we look up the reference, instead of this being a reason for eating a boar, this incident caused some *not* to eat it:

> Hermesianax...says that Attis was a son of Calaus, a Phrygian, and that he was a eunuch from his mother's womb. When he grew up he migrated...to Lydia, and celebrated the orgies of the Mother for the Lydians, who honored him so highly that Zeus, incensed at him, sent a boar to ravage the fields of the Lydians. Thereupon Attis and some of the Lydians were slain by the boar, and in consequence of this the Galatians of Pessinus *abstain* from swine.[2]

In another story cited by Hislop, a boar killed Adonis, whom he takes to be the same as Attis or Tammuz.[3] But when the boar was brought in chains to Venus, it pleaded so pathetically that the killing was an accident, she forgave it.[4] In the accompanying drawing, said to be of the Emperor Trajan burning incense to the goddess Diana, Hislop draws attention to the head of a *boar* in the tree. Despite the disjointed nature of these examples,  Hislop concludes: "Hence the boar's head is still a standing dish in England at the Christmas dinner"![5] We find ourselves asking: Where is the connection?

CHRISTMAS GOOSE

Next, Hislop tries to explain another custom among the English: eating the "Christmas goose." For this he cites examples that take us on a real goose chase! He mentions that geese, sacred to Juno,

---

1. Hislop, p. 99, 100.   2. Pausanias' *Description of Greece*, Book 7, chap. 17.   3. Hislop, p. 99.   4. Ibid., p. 100.   5. Ibid., p. 101.

were kept in the temple of Jupiter at Rome. And, he includes two drawings: the Egyptian god Seb with a goose on his head and a sacrificial goose on a stand.[1]

Concerning the drawing shown below, Hislop says it "proves that the goose in Asia Minor was the symbol of Cupid."[2] But when we actually look up the reference he gives,[3] it is not quite that clear. The writer shows a drawing titled: "Cupid and Swan," and says "the association of Cupid and the swan was very common." He does question whether

the neck of the bird in the drawing is long enough to represent a swan's, but says nothing about a "goose." He then presents the drawing reproduced here—from a terra-cotta image found in *Italy* (not Asia Minor)—comparing the two birds, which are similar in appearance. Was this drawing intended to represent Cupid riding a goose? From the text it is unclear. But, assuming this was the case, what would it prove?

Suppose a turkey was worshipped or sacrificed by an ancient tribe. Suppose we could reproduce an old drawing of Tammuz with a turkey on his head, or Tammuz riding on a turkey. Would this have any bearing on why Americans eat turkey at Thanksgiving? Hislop's evidence is no stronger than this.

The way Hislop connects eating the goose with Christmas is by quoting Wilkinson—that in Egypt the "goose" could not be eaten "except in the *depth of winter*."[4] Finally, it would seem, Hislop is zeroing in on the point—that Egyptians must have had

1. Hislop, p. 101   2. Ibid., pp. 101, 102.   3. Barker, *Lares and Penates,* chap. 4, p. 220.   4. Hislop, p. 101.

some pagan celebration that corresponded to Christmas—at which time they ate a goose. But when we turn to the reference and see what it actually says, again the quote does not fit the claim! Writing over 150 years ago, when there was no refrigeration, Wilkinson said: "In Egypt, *and similar climates,* beef *and* goose are not eligible food, *except in the depth of winter.*"[1] The careful reader will notice it was not just Egypt that was referred to, but also other places with a hot climate; it was not just goose, but also beef that would spoil, and so was eaten only in the depth of winter. This had nothing to do with a Christmas custom.

Hislop's criticism about Easter eggs is equally weak. "In ancient times eggs were used in the religious rites of the Egyptians and the Greeks," he says, "and were hung up for mystic purposes in their temples."[2] In checking the references he cites, one was a rite involving, specifically, an *ostrich* egg,[3] and the other mentions a sanctuary of Hilaira and Phoebe, where an egg, believed to be the famous egg Leda gave birth to, was hung by ribbons from the roof.[4] There is nothing in these references that would parallel today's seasonal use of decorated eggs. If at some other time and place there were people who *worshipped* eggs, this is not the case now.[5]

"Besides the mystic egg," Hislop continues, "there was also another emblem of Easter, the goddess queen of Babylon, and that was the rimmon or 'pomegranate'."[6] He gives the accompanying drawing of Juno, holding in one hand a pomegranate, and in the other a cuckoo.[7] He spares us the details about the cuckoo—"into the story of the cuckoo I cannot enter here"[8]—but seeks to put the pomegranate, along with eggs and even *oranges,*[9] in a bad light. But what is the point? He fails to mention that pomegranates also decorated the pillars in front of the Temple (1 Kings 7:20) and the robe of the High Priest (Exod. 39:24).

1. Wilkinson, *Ancient Egyptians,* vol. 2, p. 380.   2. Hislop, p. 109.   3. Wilkinson, vol. 3, p. 20.   4. Pausanias, Book 3, chapter 16.   5. For a more complete study, see my two 64-page booklets: *Easter—Is it Pagan?* and *Christmas—Reconsidered.* Catalog available upon request.   6. Hislop, p. 110.   7. Ibid., p. 111.   8. Ibid.   9. Ibid., p. 113.

Chapter Eight

PAGAN CONNECTION?

Finding pagan similarities has caused some to condemn innocent things—even the traditional American Thanksgiving! They point out that ancient people held festivals in the autumn to give thanks for a bountiful harvest, citing references about the Romans who did so in honor of Ceres, goddess of grains.[1]

Others, if they wanted to put down "Mother's Day," could quote the following line from the *People's Almanac,* "The beginnings of this holiday may have been in the ancient spring festival known as Hilaria, dedicated to the mother goddess Cybele."[2] But there is no connection. Mother's Day, as we know it, stems from the efforts of a Miss Jarvis and others who promoted the idea, and which was made official on May 9, 1914, by a proclamation of President Woodrow Wilson. It is not a pagan day, it is a day to honor mothers, and has no connection with the goddess Cybele!

I know of several churches that have set aside a day each year which they call "Friend's Day." Members, as a result, can say to others: "We are having 'Friend's Day' at our church; we would like you to attend as our friend." A pastor I have known for many years, told me that people in his church became involved in this, resulting in a record attendance. The goal, of course, is not merely to set an attendance record, but to share the gospel of Jesus Christ. Technically, there is no Biblical command that says: "Each year thou shalt have Friend's Day." But does there need to be? We can judge such things by their *fruits.*

1. Hatch, *The American Book of Days,* p. 1053.   2. Wallechinsky, *People's Almanac,* p. 939.

Many things we do are not spelled out in the Bible—things like the time we have services, how long the services last, how many songs we sing, the type of building we worship in, what musical instruments we use, whether the church should have a radio or TV ministry, and a whole host of other things. Should a central position be given to the pulpit, or the communion table? Should we use hymnals, or overhead projection? Should we have a song leader, or a worship team? Should the organ be on the platform, or screened away from view? Should people stand to pray, or kneel? Should people come forward to receive communion, or be served by ushers? The Bible gives no rigid rules about such things, all of which fall within the framework of Christian liberty.

Christians who suppose they need "chapter and verse" from the Bible for everything they do, may be surprised to learn that the words "chapter," "verse," and "Bible" are not in the Bible! The reason is quite simple: chapters and verses were added centuries later! The word "Bible" did not appear as a title for the complete Christian Scriptures until the 5th century.[1] According to *Harper's Bible Dictionary*, "Byblos (the Phoenician city from which the word 'Bible' is derived) was for centuries a center of Adonis worship similar to that of Tammuz."[2] So, what are we to do? Waste time preaching against the word "Bible"?

We are all familiar with hymns that rhyme, like:

Amazing grace how sweet the SOUND,
That saved a wretch like ME,
I once was lost, but now am FOUND,
Was blind but now I SEE.

Yet, according to *A Short History of Music,* the now-common practice of using rhyme in hymns was unknown to the early Christians and was a custom that developed later.[3]

I know a man who once belonged to a religious group that was so strict against having anything "added," they would not sing any of the great hymns written in recent centuries. They sang only words that are *in the Bible.* Perhaps they did not realize they were

---

1. *Hastings' Bible Dictionary,* article: "Bible."   2. *Harper's Bible Dictionary,* Article: "Tammuz."   3. Einstein, *A Short History of Music,* p. 15.

still adding something: *the tune!* No musical notes are printed in the Bible.

Some have quoted the statement of Moses, "You shall not *add* unto the word which I command you" (Deut. 4:2) as though it meant that only those things actually spelled out in the Bible are valid. On this basis, one group refused to eat potatoes or tomatoes —because they are not mentioned in the Bible!

When Moses told the Israelites not to add to the word he commanded them, it must be understood in context. It cannot mean God had no further revelation to his people—beyond what Moses said—for then Deuteronomy would have been the last book in the Bible! Indeed, this is the error the Samaritans fell into, believing no books added after Deuteronomy were authoritative.[1] Consequently, they taught that Mount Ebal was where men should worship God (Deut. 27:4); while the Jews, accepting the later books of the Bible, placed their focus on Jerusalem (2 Chron. 7:12). This difference prompted the Samaritan woman at the well to say to Jesus: "Our fathers worshipped in this mountain; and you say that in Jerusalem is the place where men ought to worship" (John 4:20). The reply of Jesus, surpassing details about a geographical location, pointed out that God is a Spirit and those who worship him must do so in spirit and in truth.

If a pastor could add nothing to the Bible, his sermons would consist only of reading or reciting the Bible. He could not give his personal testimony of what God has done in his life, yet—in the Bible—Paul repeatedly did this! The pastor's sermons could not give any contemporary illustrations, yet Jesus and the apostles—in the Bible—commonly did this: a farmer sowing seed, shepherds tending sheep, men who run in a race, soldiers preparing for battle, a wayward son, the rudder on a ship, etc. It is strange to say, but there is a danger for some, like the Pharisees of old, of becoming so strict about always being Biblical, they become un-biblical.

Make no mistake about it, nothing can be added as far as salvation is concerned; clearly this is found in Christ (Acts 4:12). "For other foundation can no man lay than that is laid, which is

---

1. *Hastings' Bible Dictionary,* article: "Bible."

Jesus Christ" (1 Cor. 3:11), yet *on this foundation,* we do build. The wrong is not that we build, but *how* we build, as Paul explains (verses 10-15). Following the Day of Pentecost, things were added, a notable example being the missionary outreach to Gentiles that developed (Acts 11:18). Even that portion of the Bible that we call the New Testament was added after Pentecost!

Rather than hastily condemning a practice as *wrong* because it is not spelled out in the Bible, it would be better to ask: Is it spiritually fruitful? Does it glorify Christ? Is it in harmony with the Bible? If not, then of course it should be discarded along with anything that is truly pagan.

By citing pagan similarities, the Bible itself could be condemned as being "pagan."

KNEELING. In Babylon, pagans bowed before an image set up by Nebuchadnezzar, and bowing the knees was clearly a part of Baal worship (Dan. 3:7; 1 Ki 19:18). *In the Bible,* Daniel knelt and prayed to the true God, and Paul said, "I bow my knees unto the Father of our Lord Jesus Christ" (Dan. 6:10; Eph 3:14).

UPRAISED HANDS. The accompanying illustration, from an Egyptian grotto, shows two pagan priests worshipping a sun-image with upraised hands.[1] Lucian spoke of worshipping "The Unknown God" at Athens "with our hands stretched up to heaven"[2] (cf. Acts 17:23). A line from Virgil reads:

> Amidst the statues of the gods he stands,
> Spreading forth to Jove his lifted hands.[3]

In the Bible, the custom of raising hands in the worship of God is repeatedly mentioned—verses like, "Lift up your hands in the sanctuary" (Ps. 134:2) and, "Pray every where, lifting up holy hands" (1 Tim. 2:8).

1. Hislop, p. 162.   2. Original sources cited in *Clarke's Commentary,* vol. 5, p. 826.
3. Ibid., vol. 1, p. 337.

A drawing of the familiar "pray-ing hands" is widely recognized as a symbol of prayer. But some "claim" even this goes all the way back to a pagan practice of binding the hands to show submission to various gods or masters!

BAREFOOTED. The ancient Greeks, as mentioned by Jamblichus, offered sacrifices and worshipped with their shoes off. Solinus asserts that no person was permitted to enter into the temple of Diana, in Crete, until he had removed his shoes. This is also the practice of Muslims at the Dome of the Rock in Jerusalem. Tertullian mentioned worshippers of Jupiter who prayed for rain walking barefooted.[1] *In the Bible,* God told Moses to take off his shoes for he was standing on holy ground (Exod. 3:5).

CEREMONY. According to Kitto, often quoted by Hislop, "many nations of antiquity had a practice of binding themselves to certain resolutions by the ceremony of cutting a calf or other victim into two halves...and passing between the severed parts."[2] *In the Bible,* this was the same custom that Abraham followed in receiving a solemn promise from God (Gen. 15:9-17; see also Jer. 34:18,19).

HOLY MOUNTAIN. Pagans had their holy mountains, one being Mount Ida, mentioned by Ovid.[3] *In the Bible,* concepts about a "holy mount" or "holy mountain" were held by Israelites and are described in these very terms (Is. 27:13; Dan. 9:20; 2 Pet. 1:18).

HOLY PLACE. The pagans had in the inmost part of their temples a holy place to which none had access but the priests.[4] An ancient temple at Asswan, Egypt, which I have personally seen, is an example of this. *In the Bible,* the Temple at Jerusalem had a holy of holies into which only the high priest could enter (Heb. 9:25).

1. Original sources cited in *Clarke's Commentary,* vol. 1, p. 304.   2. Kitto, *Cyclopaedia of Biblical Literature,* Article: "Calf."   3. Hislop, p. 72.   4. Clarke, vol. 1, p. 435.

PRIESTS. Priests who served in the ancient temple of Hercules, "were always clothed in fine linen, and their bonnets made of the same....and kept a perpetual fire burning on their altars."[1] *In the Bible,* Israelite priests were clothed in fine linen and wore linen bonnets (Exod. 39:27,28). Fires were kept continually burning on the altar (Lev. 6:13).

TEMPLE PILLARS. Pagan temples, such as those among the Phoenicians, were known to include two large pillars in front.[2] *In the Bible,* Solomon's temple also had two large pillars in front of it (2 Chron. 3:17).

WITHOUT BLEMISH. Pagan Egyptians, as Herodotus mentions, went to great lengths to make certain the white bulls sacrificed to their god Apis were without any blemish.[3] *In the Bible,* the Israelites were repeatedly told to offer sacrifices that were "without blemish" (Lev. 22:19, etc.).

VICARIOUS SACRIFICE. When sacrificing a bull to Apis, the Egyptians believed that "any evil hanging over them or the land of Egypt" was transferred to the head of the animal, which they either sold to the Greeks or threw into the Nile.[4] *In the Bible,* Israelites had a ritual whereby sins were transferred to the head of a goat (Lev. 16:21).

SACRED ARKS. Tacitus tells how in the north of Germany, Hertham, the mother earth, was worshipped. A sacred ark, within which she was supposed to reside, and which could be touched only by priests, was drawn by cows.[5] *In the Bible,* the ark of God, pulled by oxen, was likewise restricted from touching (1 Chron. 13:9, 10).

CITY OF REFUGE. The idea of a "city of refuge" to which an accused person could flee for his life was known among pagans. One such site may be visited at the City of Refuge National Historical Park on the Big Island of Hawaii. *In the Bible,* cities of refuge are mentioned numerous times (Num. 35:11-14, etc.).

---

1. *Clarke's Commentary,* vol. 1, p. 442.   2. *Hastings' Dictionary of the Bible,* article: "Jachin and Boaz."   3. Clarke, vol. 1, pp. 559, 560.   4. Ibid., p. 562.   5. Ibid., p. 435.

THRONES. Pagan kings sat on thrones (Esther 5:1). *In the Bible*, Israelite kings sat on thrones and even the Lord is pictured as sitting on a throne (Psalms 47:8).

LIONS. The walls bordering Babylon's Procession Street from the Ishtar Gate to the Temple of Marduk were adorned with the famous sixty lions (sacred to Ishtar).[1] *In the Bible*, Solomon's ivory throne, with a series of steps leading up to it, was elaborately decorated with statues of twelve lions (1 Kings 10:18-20).

HEALING. Isis, a prominent Egyptian goddess, was believed to be the preventer or healer of all diseases.[2] *In the Bible*, the Israelites, having just fled from Egypt, believed the *Lord* was the preventer and healer of all diseases (Exod. 15:26).

FATAL VISION. In mythology, Semelé begged Jupiter to show her his glory, but he hesitated, knowing this would be fatal to her. But when she persisted, he appeared to her in his divine majesty and she was consumed by his presence.[3] *In the Bible*, the Israelites also believed that if they were to see God in his glory, they could not survive (Exod. 33:20, etc.).

ROD. In pagan fable, the god Mercury used a rod whereby he performed many miracles, to which Homer refers.[4] *In the Bible*, Moses with a rod in his hand performed many miracles in Egypt (Exod. 4:17).

WATER FROM ROCK. In pagan fable, the goddess Rhea struck a rock and brought forth water. A Greek poet expressed it in these words:

> With her sceptre struck
> the yawning cliff;
> from its disparted height
> adown the mount
> the gushing torrent ran.[5]

In the Bible, God told Moses: "...thou shalt smite the rock, and there shall come water out of it" (Exod. 17:6).

1. *Harper's Bible Dictionary*, article: "Lion," p. 396.   2. *Clarke's Commentary*, vol. 1, p. 361.   3. Ovid, *Metamorphosis*, book 3, fable 3, 5.   4. Clarke, vol. 1, p. 311.   5. Ibid., p. 389.

LAWS ON STONE. The famous law code of Hammurabi was written on stone. *In the Bible,* the Ten Commandments were also written on tables of stone (Exod. 31:18).

FIRE. There were pagans—the Prometheus-worshipping Greeks, the Persians who worshipped the son of Ahura Mazda, and the cultists of Mithraism—who associated fire with deity.[1] *In the Bible,* the Israelites believed God revealed himself in a pillar of fire and a burning bush (Ps. 78:14; Exod. 3:2).

FIRE ON HEAD. Adam Clarke says: "A flame of fire seen upon the head of any person was, among the heathens, considered as an omen from their gods that the person was under the peculiar care of a supernatural power, and destined to some extraordinary employment. Many proofs of this occur in the Roman poets and historians."[2] He then cites lines from Virgil:

> Strange to relate! from young Iulus' *head,*
> A *lambent flame* arose, which gently spread
> Around his brows, and on his temples fed.
> Amazed, with running water, we prepare
> To quench the sacred fire, and slake his hair.[3]

In the Bible, when the disciples were filled with the Holy Spirit on the Day of Pentecost, "there appeared unto them cloven tongues like as of *fire,* and it sat upon each of them"! (Acts 2:3).

HORSES OF FIRE. In pagan mythology, Apollo was seated in a blazing chariot, drawn by horses which breathed and snorted fire. These horses were four, and called Pyroeis, Eous, Aethon, and Phlegon—names all linked with fire.[4] *In the Bible,* when Elijah was taken up into heaven, there appeared a "chariot of fire, and horses of fire" (2 Kings 2:11).

FEAST OF TABERNACLES. Plutarch supposed the Jews worshiped the god Bacchus, "because he had a feast of exactly the same kind called the feast of tabernacles, which they celebrated in the time of vintage, bringing tables out into the open air furnished with all kinds of fruit, and sitting under tents made of vine branches and ivy."[5]

---

1. *Harper's Bible Dictionary,* article: "Fire." 2. *Clarke's Commentary,* vol. 5, p. 692. 3. Ibid., p. 693. 4. Ibid., vol. 2, p. 484. 5. Ibid., vol. 1, p. 587.

FIRSTFRUITS. Pliny attests that the pagan Romans never tasted either their new corn or wine, till the priests had offered the first-fruits to the gods.[1] *In the Bible,* the Israelites offered their first-fruits to God (Lev. 23:10).

If we build on similarities, ignoring differences, nearly anything can be made out to be pagan. Atheists have used the same method, rejecting the Bible altogether, supposing its writers borrowed their ideas from paganism. But in many cases, *it was the other way around.* Adam Clarke, from whom many of the references mentioned here were gleaned, says pagans often borrowed from events and practices recorded *in the Bible.* This point was also emphasized by Tertullian.[2]

If we base conclusions on similarities alone, not only the Bible, but the Lord himself would be pagan!

The pagan "woman" called "Mystery Babylon" had a cup in her hand; the Lord has a cup in his hand (Psa. 75:8).

Pagan kings sat on thrones and wore crowns; the Lord sits on a throne and wears a crown (Rev. 1:4; 14:14).

Pagans worshipped the sun; the Lord is the "Sun of righteousness" (Mal. 4:2).

Pagan gods were likened to stars; the Lord is called "the bright morning star" (Rev. 22:16).

Pagan gods had temples dedicated to them; the Lord has a temple (Rev. 7:15).

Pagans built a high tower in Babylon; the Lord is a high tower (2 Sam. 22:3).

Pagan gods were pictured with wings; the Lord is pictured with wings (Psa. 91:4).

Janus, "the god of doors and hinges," was represented with a "key," and called Patulcius and Clusius, "the opener and shutter."[3] But the Lord Jesus, speaking to the church at Philadelphia in Asia Minor—as though to counter this—says *He* has a "key" and that *He "opens,* and no man shuts, and shuts, and no man opens" (Rev.

1. *Clarke's Commentary,* vol. 1, p. 417.   2. Ibid., vol. 1, p. 441.   3. Hislop, p. 210.

3:7). Pagans may have regarded Janus as their opener and shutter, but to Christians, the true opener and shutter is Jesus Christ!

In each of these examples there is a *similarity*—but the *differences* are AWESOME! Primitive men may have worshipped a rock, but as a Biblical writer put it, *"Their rock is not as our Rock"*! (Deut. 32:31).

Citing a pagan parallel may not provide conclusive evidence, for sometimes pagans held opposite beliefs.

We might assume that all pagans made idols, but in fact some pagans *opposed* making idols. Tacitus, writing in 98 A.D., spoke of Germans offering sacrifices to gods such as Mercury, Hercules, and Mars. But "their deities are not immured in temples, nor represented under any kind of resemblance to the human form. To do either, would, in their opinion, derogate from the majesty of superior beings."[1] If "everything" pagans did was wrong, then—based on this example—*"not* making an idol" would be wrong!

Some practices are so general they provide no proof of pagan origins.

Suppose someone criticized a brick church building, arguing that *bricks* came from Babylon: "And they said one to another, Go to, let us make brick, and burn them throughly" (Gen. 11:3). But the use of bricks is too general to make a Babylonian connection. Would a wood-frame building, covered with plaster, be less Babylonian? Well, no, for the Babylonians also used plaster! (Dan. 5:5).

The Babylonians represented Shamash, the sun-god, as riding in a chariot.[2] But this could not make chariots "pagan," for such was a general practice. When Philip encountered the Ethiopian official returning from Jerusalem in a chariot, he did not waste time preaching about the paganism of chariots! He had something better to preach: Jesus Christ! (Acts 8:35).

According to Diodorus, when Semiramis marched into Media and Persia, she ordered that mountains be cut down and hollows filled up, so that at great expense she made a shorter road which was

1. Tacitus, *Germania* IX.   2. *Hastings' Bible Dictionary,* article: "Chariot."

called "The Road of Semiramis."[1] Today modern highway construction is done the same way— high places are cut down and the low places are filled in. Are we, then, going to argue that highways are "pagan" because this was the practice of Semiramis?

If general practices are any proof of paganism, one could even argue that eating Chinese food is evil, as the following spoof, gleaned from "The Menace of Chinese Food," demonstrates:

> Chinese food is not mentioned in the New Testament, so it is *unscriptural*. It came from the East, so it is *pagan*. Unlike a plate of food in the West—consisting of separate portions —Chinese food commonly has salad, vegetables, meats, and sweets *mixed* together. It must be an idolatrous mixture, as proven by the fact that people, even being warned, still continue to eat it! *Many* non-Christians eat Chinese food. Anything that many people do must be *evil!*

> Few modern Christians have studied the classic exposé of Chinese food by Alexander Slipshod: *The Four Babylons.* Slipshod in his masterful work demonstrates beyond a shadow of doubt that Chinese food originated at the Tower of Babel, Nimrod and three of his cousins...known as the 'gang of four,' developed Chinese food as a subtle means of undermining the true faith....Slipshod shows that it was the Bishop of Rome who introduced Chinese food into the Christian world...a Romish plot![2]

Some practices are so limited they provide no proof regarding pagan origins.

Hislop tells of a rite performed by a midwife in Mexico, at the time of Cortez. She sprinkled water on the head of an infant, with the idea that the drops would enter the body and remove sin, such being done with the blessing of Chalchivitlycue (goddess of water). This was performed at early dawn, in the decorated courtyard of a house, while the woman faced west, etc. Hislop cites this as an example of how Babylonian religion spread to "the Mexicans."[3] But what was only a localized practice, hardly justifies this sweeping statement as though this was a widespread custom all over Mexico.

---

1. *Clarke's Commentary,* vol. 5, p. 51.   2. Jordan, "The Menace of Chinese Food," in *Presbyterian Heritage,* December 1984.   3. Hislop, p. 133, 134.

If a visitor to the United States heard about people handling snakes in some backwoods area of Kentucky, it would be misleading if he returned home and said: "Christians in America handle snakes!" This would *not* accurately describe the overall practice of Christians in America. And, it would become even more disjointed if he said they got the idea from Nimrod, who "introduced the worship of the serpent,"[1] citing Hislop as his source!

Often arguments about pagan origins are based on similarities, but without any real connection.

Let's suppose that on May 10th a man was stabbed to death in Seattle. There were strong reasons for believing a certain person did it. He had motive. He was physically strong. He owned a large knife. He had a criminal record. He was known to have a violent temper and had threatened the victim in the past. All of these things would connect him to the murder, except for one thing: on May 10th he was not in Seattle—he was in Florida! So is it with the claims that are made about pagan origins. They may *seem* to have a connection, but upon further investigation, often there is no connection at all!

It has been said that blowing out candles with a single puff in order for a wish to come true "was originally a rite to gain the favor of the goddess Artemis."[2]
If this is correct, it would not mean a person today who blows out candles believes in Artemis! That meaning is obsolete. Without a belief in Artemis, there is no connection.

Let's turn it around. Suppose a remote tribe practiced water baptism, but did not know it represented the death, burial, and resurrection of Jesus Christ. Without faith in Christ, the rite itself would not make them *Christians*. By the same token, if some blow out candles on a cake, this does not make them *pagans*.

1. Hislop, p. 298.   2.Maple, *Origins: Superstitions and their Meanings*, p. 8.

To believe there is connection when there is none, is only superstition.

A man once told me his mother, living in a Louisiana swamp area, would not keep a broom in the house. She apparently associated brooms with witches. But where is the connection? For most people a broom is simply a broom. Even the Lord is pictured as having a broom! (Isa. 14:23). There is no connection between "fathers eating sour grapes," and "the children's teeth being set on edge" (cf. Ezek. 18:2; Jer. 31:29). There is no connection between bad luck and a black cat. There is no connection between good luck and a rabbit's foot. The rabbit's foot didn't help the rabbit!

Let's face it, by mixing facts and fables together, nearly anything can be made to appear "pagan," as the following will illustrate:

Do you suppose those "Golden Arches" at McDonald's restaurant really stand for the M in the name McDonald's? The arch was known in the land of *Babylon* from ancient times, dating back as early as 2020 B.C.[1] The accompanying illustration, from Layard, is described as "the king standing in an *arched* frame."[2] Now, as is well-known, Nebuchadnezzar set up a *"golden* image" to be worshipped in Babylon

(Dan. 3:5-10), and Babylon itself was called *"the golden* city" (Isa. 14:4). Can there be the slightest doubt, then, that Babylon had golden arches?

Is it a mere coincidence that a double arch forms the letter M—the 13th letter of the alphabet—13 being widely regarded as an unlucky and *occult* number. After the M, counting to the end of the alphabet, the remaining letters number exactly 13! For what does the letter M stand? Let one who was initiated into the Chaldean mysteries gaze upon it and immediately he knows the M stands for Moloch, the fire-god (Lev. 18:21).

1. *The Encyclopedia Americana,* article: "Arch."   2. Layard, *Babylon and Nineveh,* p. 160.

Who else could Moloch be but Nimrod, who taught fire worship in Babylon? If we add the number of letters in "Babylon" and "Nimrod" together they total 13. If any more proof be needed, consider that Nimrod was the *king* of Babylon. "Molech" signifies *king*—the king of heaven or the sun. And the sun has a *golden* color!

Now Nimrod, who in his mystery form was none other than the fish-god Dagon, must have worn the fish-head mitre. "Mitre" begins with M, and even its shape resembles the M. We must not overlook the fact that the word "Mystery"—the Chaldean Mysteries being started by Nimrod—also begins with an M, as does the word "Masonic"!

From ancient Babylon, the arch later came to Rome. There, to this day, the best preserved monument of ancient Rome is the Arch of *Constantine,* erected in 315 A.D., a clear indication of the Romish nature of memorial arches. It should be kept in mind, also, it was Constantine who presided at the *Nicene Council* just ten years later!

Now it is well-known that McDonald's has served billions of hamburgers, requiring a large quantity of beef. When the Israelites came out of Egypt, they worshipped a calf. And what was its color? It was a *"golden* calf " (Exod. 32:3, 4)! Can there be any doubt, then, as to the Babylonish origin of golden arches?

The stupidity of this mixture of facts and fable should be apparent to all. Such is the inconsistency of producing a *mixture* of disconnected facts, myths, and misinformation—to prove we should not have a *mixture!*

Chapter Nine

EXCESS BAGGAGE

The Pope is *Nimrod's* representative,[1] Hislop says, the head of Devil-worship, "to bring ALL its abominations into the Church, as he has done."[2] Has the Pope brought ALL the abominations of Devil-worship into the Church? When Hislop makes extreme statements such as this, he unfortunately discredits his valid points.

Hislop says of the Roman Catholic Church, its doctrines and discipline "in ALL essential respects, have been derived from Babylon," and that it teaches "ALL that is dishonoring to the Most High, and ruinous to the moral and spiritual welfare of mankind."[3] It would be more appropriate to say that "some" things that have been taught in the Roman Catholic Church dishonor God and are ruinous to the moral and spiritual welfare of mankind. The word "all," in this context, is inappropriate. Despite the "excess baggage" it has accumulated over the centuries, the Roman Catholic Church teaches many things that are honorable and moral.

Instead of using a sweeping statement that the Roman Catholic Church (or some other group) is wrong on "all" it teaches, it would be better to find areas of agreement, establish some common ground, and build from there. This was Paul's approach, even when dealing with those who were undeniably *pagans*. At Athens, the common ground he pointed out was that both pagans and Christians conceived of God as the Creator of mankind, one who is omnipresent: "For in him we live, and move, and have our being; *as certain also of your own poets have said,* For we are his offspring" (Acts 17:28). One of the Greek poets to whom Paul referred, Aratus, had written the following words about 300 years before:

1. Hislop, p. 269.   2. Ibid., p. 281.   3. Ibid., p. 129.

With Jove we must begin; nor from him rove;
Him always praise, for all is full of Jove!
He fills all places where mankind resort,
The wide-spread sea, with every shelt'ring port.
Jove's presence fills all space....
For we his offspring are; and he in love,
Points out to man his labor from above.[1]

Back over the ages, as men have sought to fill the spiritual vacuum in their lives—even though they were pagans—they were not wrong on "everything." It should be no surprise, then, that there are similarities in some things—even between pagans and Christians.

We should also keep in mind that Roman Catholics and evangelical Christians hold a number of *major* beliefs in common. Both believe in God Almighty, Creator of heaven and earth. Both believe in His Son, the Lord Jesus Christ—that He was conceived by the Holy Spirit and born of the virgin Mary, that He was crucified, was buried, and rose again. Both believe He ascended into heaven, and that He will come again to judge the living and the dead. Both believe that Christ loved the church and gave Himself for it, providing the forgiveness of sins and life everlasting. Compared to the ideologies of a secular society, these are indeed major beliefs that are held in common!

There are also distinct differences between Roman Catholics and evangelical Christians—in doctrine, interpretation, and emphasis—things like transubstantiation, the use of statues, bowing before a communion wafer, repetitious prayers, confession to a priest, indulgences, purgatory, the perpetual virginity of Mary, forbidding priests to marry, the papacy, papal infallibility, etc.

But we have come to see that citing pagan parallels is not the best way to counter errors in the Roman Catholic Church or any other church. The better and more direct method is an appeal to the Bible itself. Whether Nimrod's wife had an order of celibate priests, for example, does not matter; the Bible argues against the doctrine of forbidding to marry. Peter, supposedly the first pope, was married (Matt. 8:14), as were the other apostles (1 Cor. 9:5). Though Paul, by choice, lived a single life (1 Cor. 7:7-9), he was an

1. Aratus, *Phaenomena,* cited in *Clarke's Commentary,* vol. 5, p. 827.

exception. He would himself write that a minister was to be "the husband of one wife" (1 Tim. 3:2), and spoke—only a few verses later—of "forbidding to marry" as a doctrine of devils! (1 Tim. 4:3).

It is evident that Peter, by the grace of God, was chosen by Christ as the leader in the opening days of the church—he presided at the meeting when Judas was replaced (Acts 1:15), he preached on the day of Pentecost when 3,000 were converted (Acts 2:14), and he was used of God to open the door of the gospel to the Gentiles (Acts 10:32). Whenever we find a list of the apostles in the Scriptures, Peter is always mentioned *first* (Matt. 10:2; Mk. 3:16; Lk. 6:14; Acts 1:13). But differences center on questions about Peter being the first pope in Rome, of leadership authority being passed on to a succession of popes, and claims about one true church being linked to this succession.

At some periods, though claiming to be the successors of Peter, there were popes that were very corrupt and immoral. *The Catholic Encyclopedia* describes John XII, for example, as "a course, immoral man, whose life was such that the Lateran was spoken of as a brothel, and the moral corruption in Rome became the subject of general odium....On 6 November a synod composed of fifty Italian and German bishops was convened in St. Peter's; John was accused of sacrilege, simony, perjury, murder, adultery, and incest, and was summoned in writing to defend himself.

"Refusing to recognize the synod, John pronounced sentence of excommunication against all participators in the assembly, should they elect in his stead another Pope....John XII took bloody vengeance on the leaders of the opposite party, Cardinal-Deacon John had his right hand struck off, Bishop Otgar of Speyer was scourged, a high palatine official lost nose and ears....John died on 14 May, 964, eight days after he had been, according to rumor, stricken by paralysis in the act of adultery."[1]

Because of such abuse of power, Protestant leaders felt compelled to emphasize in their creeds the Headship of Christ: "There is no other Head of the Church, but the Lord Jesus Christ, nor can the Pope of Rome, in any sense, be head thereof, but is that

1. *The Catholic Encyclopedia,* vol. 8, p. 426, article: "John XII."

113

Antichrist, that man of sin, and Son of Perdition, that exalteth himself in the Church."[1]

Though papal *infallibility* is technically defined within the narrow confines of "ex cathedra" pronouncements, to link infallibility in any form with this succession of men has been difficult, not only for Protestants, but some Roman Catholic leaders as well. At the Vatican Council in 1870, Roman Catholic bishop Joseph Strossmayer (1815-1905), "one of the most notable opponents of papal infallibility,"[2] made special mention of how Pope Stephen VI (896-897) brought former Pope Formosus (891-896) to trial—after Pope Formosus had been dead for eight months! As the trial got underway, the stench of the dead body filled the assembly hall. Pope Stephen did the questioning; the dead man gave no answers! The bright robes were ripped form his body, the crown from his skull, the fingers used in bestowing the pontifical blessing were hacked off, his body was dragged through the streets of Rome and cast into the  Tiber.[3] Later popes disagreed with one another as to the validity of bishops who had been "consecrated by Formosus, who in turn had meanwhile conferred orders on many other clerics, a policy which gave rise to the greatest confusion."[4]

In 1252, Pope Innocent IV issued the "Ad exstirpanda" stating that heretics should be "crushed like venomous snakes" and formally approved the use of torture. *The Catholic Encyclopedia* says this document "remained thenceforth a fundamental document of the Inquisition, renewed or reinforced by several popes, Alexander IV (1254-61), Clement IV (1265-68), Nicholas IV (1288-92), Boniface VIII (1294-1303), and others."[5] Torture instruments in various forms were used including "Spanish boots" for crushing the legs and feet, and the rack. Such actions were certainly contrary to the

1. *Westminster Confession of Faith,* chapter 25, section 6.   2. *The Catholic Encyclopedia,* vol. 14, p. 316, article: "Strossmayer."   3. Ibid., vol. 6, p. 141, article: "Formosus."   4. Ibid.   5. Ibid., vol. 8, p. 34, article: "Inquisition."

words of Jesus (Matt. 5:44) and a gross misapplication of Scripture (1 Cor. 5:5). No one today, as far as I know, would want to reopen that horrid era.

According to Roman Catholic belief, when Mary was conceived, she was in that instant "preserved exempt from all stain of original sin."[1] Yet, it is admitted that "no direct or categorical and stringent proof of the dogma can be brought forward from Scripture."[2] We believe one could go a step further and say this dogma is *contrary* to Scripture (Rom. 3:23). Mary herself said, "My spirit hath rejoiced in God my Savior" (Lk. 1:47). If from her conception she was exempt from all stain of original sin, would she need a Savior? We find this teaching unnecessary. The divinity of Jesus did not depend on his mother being a sinless person.

Certainly Mary was a godly woman, chosen of God in a unique way to be the mother of Jesus, and was blessed among women. Yet, as *The Encyclopedia Britannica* states, during the first centuries of the church, no emphasis was placed upon Mary whatsoever.[3] If indeed she was to become the Queen of Heaven, and all that this implies, we would question why there is no hint of this superiority in Scripture.

On one occasion, when his mother and brethren were mentioned, Jesus replied, "Who is my mother? and who are my brethren?" Then, stretching forth his hand toward his disciples, he said, "Behold my mother and my brethren! For *whosoever* shall do the will of my Father which is in heaven, the same is my brother, and sister, and *mother*" (Matt. 12:46-50). In a definite sense, these words position anyone who does the will of God on the same level with Mary.

In praying the Rosary, the most often repeated prayer is the "Hail Mary" which is as follows: "Hail Mary, full of grace, the Lord is with thee; Blessed art thou among women, and blessed is the fruit of thy womb, Jesus. Holy Mary, Mother of God, pray for us sinners, now and at the hour of death, Amen." The Bible does not say Mary is "full of grace," but does refer to *Jesus* in these words (John 1:14). The wording "blessed art thou among women,

1. *The Catholic Encyclopedia*, Vol. 7, p. 674, article: "Immaculate conception."   2. Ibid., p. 675.   3. *Encyclopedia Britannica*, Vol. 14, p. 309.

and blessed is the fruit of thy womb" *is* based on Scripture (Lk. 1:42). *But* the closing portion in which Mary is asked to "pray for us sinners, now and at the hour of death" places her in a position that, we feel, is contrary to Scripture (1 Tim. 2:5).

A Roman Catholic writer, Alphonsus Liguori, canonized as a "saint" by Pope Gregory XIV in 1839, described an imaginary scene in which a sinful man saw two ladders hanging from heaven. Mary was at the top of one; Jesus at the top of the other. When the sinner tried to climb the one ladder, he saw the angry face of Christ and fell defeated. But when he climbed *Mary's* ladder, he ascended easily and was openly welcomed by Mary who brought him into heaven and presented him to Christ! Then all was well. The story was supposed to show how much easier and more effective it is to go to Christ through  Mary.[1] An old woodcut (1490) included here is titled: "Jacopone da Todi before the Blessed Virgin."

In praying the Rosary, "The Lord's prayer" is included, but the prayer to Mary is repeated *many more times* than the Lord's prayer. Jesus said, "When you pray *use not vain repetitions,* as the heathen do: for they think that they shall be heard for their much speaking" (Matt. 6:7-13). Significantly, right after giving this warning, in the very next verse, Jesus said: "After this manner therefore pray: Our Father which art in heaven..."—the Lord's prayer. If *this* prayer was not to be repeated over and over, how much less a prayer directed to Mary! It seems to us that memorizing prayers, then repeating them over and over while counting rosary beads, could easily become more of a "memory test" than a spontaneous expression of prayer from the heart.

One writer has summarized the mechanical performance of a priest during Mass in these words: "He makes the sign of the cross

1. Boettner, *Roman Catholicism,* p. 147.

sixteen times; turns toward the congregation six times; lifts his eyes to heaven eleven times; kisses the altar eight times; folds his hands four times; strikes his breast ten times; bows his head twenty-one times; genuflects eight times; bows his shoulders seven times; blesses the altar with the sign of the cross thirty times; lays his hands flat on the altar twenty-nine times; prays secretly eleven times; prays aloud thirteen times; takes the bread and wine and turns it into the body and blood of Christ; covers and uncovers the chalice ten times; goes to and fro twenty times."[1] While these numbers may not be uniform at all times and places, when rituals become this routine and mechanical, it seems to us there is a danger of them becoming important in themselves, rather than that for which they were intended to stand.

If I may give a personal example, one of the ways that I pray is while walking, which may take the form of a brief walk or an extended hike. On two or three occasions, realizing that my mind was wandering from my prayer, I have picked up a little rock to carry in my hand. This served as a reminder, helping me to focus on that for which I was praying. But what if, in time, this became a doctrine: "When thou prayest, thou shalt pick up a rock"! Imagine vast numbers of people believing they needed a rock in their hands to pray! This could easily degenerate into a mere form, far removed from its original, simple, and temporary purpose.

It would be entirely proper for someone to point out the error of this practice. But if their line of argument was that it came from paganism—because some pagans worshipped rocks—this would not provide a valid connection. The better argument would simply be to show that such no longer served any fruitful purpose.

We know from the Bible itself that very early on the message of Jesus Christ impacted people who lived in Rome, even including some who were of Caesar's household (Phil. 4:22). It was a strong church that was established there, whose faith was widely known (Rom. 1:7, 8). But in time, in our opinion, this and other historic churches, became loaded down with an accumulation of excess baggage—fruitless traditions, rituals, and elaborate ceremonies —failing to maintain "the *simplicity* that is in Christ"(2 Cor 11:3).

1. Boettner, *Roman Catholicism*, p. 170.

At the time of Jesus, some of the Jews claimed they were the people of God because of a lineage back to Abraham, not realizing that God, in his miraculous sovereignty, could raise up children unto Abraham from stones (Matt. 3:9). In somewhat the same way, there are historic churches that can trace their existence back over the centuries, but have now grown cold. Consequently, from stones, as it were, God has raised up preachers who, without the unnecessary baggage of yesteryear, have effectively proclaimed the simple gospel message of Jesus Christ and brought souls to Him.

But these also face a challenge. The longer any church is in existence and the larger it grows, it becomes more vulnerable to criticism, will have had more scandals, and will include within its fold members who claim this as their church, from generations past, but who have never experienced *a personal relationship with Jesus Christ!*

God's plan for man, as outlined in the Scriptures, is that we repent of our sins, receive Jesus Christ as Savior and Lord, follow him in baptism, experience that change whereby the Holy Spirit fills our lives, empowering us for Christian service, and bringing forth fruits of love, joy, kindness, goodness, gentleness, and peace (John 1:12; Acts 1:8, 2:38; Gal 5:22). By these fruits, we believe, the people of God can be known—more than by a particular religious tag they may wear.

If the teaching about pagan origins has a positive side, it would be that it forms a *consciousness* that there can be things in our lives and churches that do not please the Lord and hinder the flow of the Holy Spirit. But, if the anti-pagan teaching is carried too far, it can have a negative and fruitless effect. Pretty soon virtually all churches are wrong—not just the Roman Catholic Church—so that one might suppose he is doing God's work by condemning churches and fellow Christians as pagans. His message to others may become: "I have no need of you" (1 Cor. 12:21). So who does he align with? Himself ?

Too long it has been said: "We saw one over here ministering in the name of Jesus, but we rejected him because he did not belong to our group." But Jesus says: "Do not reject him, he who is not against us is for us" (cf. Lk. 9:49, 50)—emphasizing the principle of inclusion, not exclusion. In following his example, we can reach out to the Samaritan woman who has suffered the heartbreak of multiple marriages, extend healing to those who are hurting, be a friend to sinners, and not shun those who may have come from a different denominational background. This is not compromise, but compassion, as we become "all things to all men" that we "might by all means save some" (1 Cor 9:22, 23).

It is our position, for the reasons we have given here, that finding a pagan similarity to a doctrine or practice does not necessarily make it wrong. There must be *connection*. Arguments based on error do not provide valid ammunition against error. Valid arguments must be factual, honest, relevant, and Scriptural. As we take a stand for truth, if we must disagree, we need not be disagreeable, "speaking the truth in love" (Eph. 4:15).

May our focus not be our buildings, programs, ceremonies, organizations, or dogmas—but *Jesus Christ* (1 Cor. 2:2). Salvation is in *Him* and not any other (Acts 4:12). *He* is Lord and wants to be Lord of our lives. It should be the desire of every believer to have more of His love, His compassion, His peace, His joy—to be drawn nearer to HIM! Fanny J. Crosby (1820-1915) expressed it well in an old hymn:

I am Thine, O Lord, I have heard Thy voice,
And it told Thy love to me;
But I long to rise in the arms of faith,
And be closer drawn to Thee.
Draw me nearer, nearer, blessed Lord,
To the cross where Thou hast died;
Draw me nearer, nearer, nearer, blessed Lord,
To Thy precious, bleeding side.

"Now the God of peace, that brought again from the dead our Lord Jesus, that Great Shepherd of the sheep, through the blood of the everlasting covenant, make you perfect in every good work to do his will, working in you that which is wellpleasing in his sight, through Jesus Christ; to whom be glory for ever and ever. Amen." (Heb. 13:20, 21).

BIBLIOGRAPHY *

Ammianus Marcellinus (c. 330—395 A.D.). *Roman History* (Cambridge: Harvard University Press, 1939).

Augustine (354—395 A.D.). *The City of God* (Chicago: William Benton, 1952).

Barker, William. *Lares and Penates* (London: Ingram, Cooke, and Company, 1853).

Boettner, Loraine. *Roman Catholicism* (Philadelphia: Presbyterian and Reformed Publishing Co., 1962).

Catholic Encyclopedia (New York: Robert Appleton Co., 1911).

Clarke, Adam. *Clarke's Commentary* (Nashville: Abingdon Press).

Eddy, Mary Baker (1821—1910). *Science and Health, with Key to the Scriptures* (Boston: Christian Scientist Publishing Co., 1875).

Einstein, Alfred. *A Short History of Music* (New York: Vintage Books, Inc., 1954).

Encyclopedia Americana (Danbury, Connecticut: Grolier Inc., 1994).

Encyclopedia Britannica (Chicago: Encyclopedia Britannica, Inc. 1985).

Encyclopedia Judaica (Jerusalem: Keter Publishing House, 1972).

Encyclopedia of Religion (New York: Macmillian Publishing Co., 1987).

Fausset's Bible Encyclopedia and Dictionary (Grand Rapids, Michigan: Zondervan).

* The bibliography for *The Babylon Connection?* has been limited to books that are quoted or referred to in the text.

Froom, *The Prophetic Faith of Our Fathers* (Washington: Review and Herald, 1945).

Grolier Encyclopedia of Knowledge (Danbury, CT: Grolier Inc., 1995).

Hastings, James (1852—1922). *Hastings' Dictionary of the Bible* (New York: Charles Scribner's Sons, 1909).

—*Hastings' Encyclopedia of Religion and Ethics* (New York: Chas. Scribner's Sons, 1928).

Harper's Bible Dictionary (New York: Harper and Row, 1961).

Hatch, Jane M. *The American Book of Days* (New York: H. W. Wilson Co., 1978).

Herodotus (c. 484 B.C.). *The History* (New York: A. A. Knopf, 1924).

Hislop, Alexander (1807—1862). *The Two Babylons* (Neptune, NJ: Loizeaux Brothers).

Irenaeus (c. 120—c. 200 A.D.). *Against Heresies* (Ante-Nicean Fathers).

Jewish Encyclopedia (New York: Funk and Wagnalls Company, 1901).

Jordan, James B. "The Menace of Chinese Food" (*Presbyterian Heritage,* December 1984).

Josephus, Flavius (c. 37—c. 100 A.D.). *Antiquities of the Jews* (Philadelphia: The John C. Winston Company, 1957).

Justin Martyr (c. 100—c. 165 A.D.). *Dialogue with Typho* (Washington: Consortium Books, 1948).

Keating, Karl. *Catholicism and Fundamentalism* (San Francisco: Ignatius Press, 1988).

Kitto, John (1804—1854). *A Cyclopedia of Biblical Literature* (Edinburgh: A. & C. Black, 1862).

Klemm, Scott. *In Search of Mystery Babylon* (Highland, CA: unpublished manuscript, 1985).

Layard, Austen Henry (1817—1894). *Nineveh and its Remains* (London: J. Murray, 1849).

—*Nineveh and Babylon* (London: J. Murray, 1853).

Maple, Eric. *Origins: Superstitions and their Meanings* (Pleasantville, NY: The Reader's Digest Association, Inc., 1978).

McPherson, Aimee (1890—1944). *This is That* (Los Angeles: The Bridal Call, 1919).

Monaghan, Patricia. *Goddesses and Heroines* (Llewellyn Pub., 1981).

New Illustrated Bible Dictionary (Nashville: Thomas Nelson, 1995).

New Catholic Encyclopedia (New York: McGraw-Hill, 1967).

New Century Classical Handbook (New York: Appleton-Century-Crofts, Inc., 1962).

Ovid (43 B.C.—17 A.D.). *Metamorphosis* (Baltimore: The John Hopkins University Press, 1994).

Pausanias (143—176 A.D.). *Pausanias' Description of Greece* (London: Macmillan and Co., 1913).

Petrie, Flinders. *Decorative Patterns of the Ancient World* (New York, Dover Publications, Inc. 1974).

Pulpit Commentary (Grand Rapids: Wm. B. Eerdmans, 1950).

Seventh-day Adventist Commentary (Washington: Review and Herald, 1957).

Silberger Jr., Julius. *Mary Baker Eddy—An Interpretive Biography of the Founder of Christian Science* (Boston: Little and Brown, 1980).

Skeat, Walter W. *A Concise Etymological Dictionary of the English Language* (New York: Capricorn Books, 1963).

Strong, James. *Strong's Concordance of the Bible* (Nashville: Abingdon Press).

Tacitus, Cornelius (c. 56—c. 120 A.D.). *The Histories—Germania* (New York: The Modern Library, 1942).

Theological Wordbook of the Old Testament (Chicago: The Moody Bible Institute, 1980).

Tyack, George S. *Historic Dress of the Clergy* (London: William Andrews and Co., 1897).

Unger, Merrill F. *Unger's Bible Dictionary* (Chicago: Moody Press, 1981).

Vine, W.E. *An Expository Dictionary of New Testament Words* (Westwood, New Jersey: Revell, 1940).

Wallechinsky, David. *People's Almanac* (Garden City, NY: Doubleday and Co., 1975).

White, Arthur. *Ellen G. White, Messenger to the Remnant* (Washington: Review and Herald Publishing Association, 1969).

White, Ellen G. (1826—1915). *The Great Controversy* (Mountain View, California: Pacific Press Publishing Association, 1911).

Wilkinson, Sir John Gardner (1797—1875). *Manners and Customs of the Ancient Egyptians* (London: J. Murray, 1837).

Worldbook Encyclopedia (Chicago: World Book, Inc., 1991).

In addition to *THE BABYLON CONNECTION?* three other books by Ralph Woodrow contain information on the subject of pagan mixture—

"THREE DAYS AND THREE NIGHTS"— *RECONSIDERED IN LIGHT OF SCRIPTURE*

Is Good Friday pagan? Why do 20 Bible verses use the term "in three days" or "the third day," and only *one* "three days and three nights"? Was a time element the *only* sign Jesus gave that He was the Messiah? (64 pages).

CHRISTMAS—RECONSIDERED

Was Nimrod the first Santa Claus? Should the celebration of Christmas be rejected because it is not mentioned in the Bible? Does "mas" in the word "Christmas" give it a Roman Catholic meaning? Was Christ born in winter? Shepherds did not "abide in the fields" in winter—*or did they?* Did Jeremiah condemn Christmas trees? (64 pages).

EASTER—IS IT PAGAN?

Is "Easter" the name of a pagan goddess? Did Constantine start Easter at the Nicene Council? Are eggs and rabbits evil symbols? Is decorating Easter eggs a pagan fertility rite? Are Easter sunrise services Baal worship? (64 pages).

For a catalog of books and tapes, contact:

RALPH WOODROW
P. O. Box 21,
PALM SPRINGS, CA   92263-0021   USA

Toll free order line: (877) 664-1549
Fax: (760) 323-3982
Email: ralphwoodrow@earthlink.net
Website: www.ralphwoodrow.org